LAW OF THE HEART

GIRGUS, SAM B.

This is an authorized facsimile, made from the master copy of the original book.

Out-of-Print Books on Demand is a publishing service of UMI. The program offers xerographic reprints of more than 100,000 books that are no longer in print.

The primary focus is academic and professional resource materials originally published by university presses, academic societies and trade book publishers worldwide.

The Law of the Heart

Sam B. Girgus

The Law of the Heart
Individualism and the Modern
Self in American Literature

University of Texas Press, Austin & London

The publication of this book was assisted by a grant from the Andrew W. Mellon Foundation.

Library of Congress Cataloging in Publication Data
Girgus, Sam B   1941–
    The law of the heart.
    Includes bibliographical references and index.
    1. American literature—History and criticism.
2. Individualism in literature.   3. Personality and
culture.   4. United States—Civilization—20th century.   I. Title.
PS169.I53G5   810'.9   78-24340
ISBN 0-292-74622-9

DEDICATED TO JOEL

August 24, 1931–December 6, 1977

Contents

Contents

Acknowledgments

During various phases of this book's development I have been inordinately fortunate in receiving help of a decisive nature from several people who read the manuscript in its entirety and offered comments that now serve to make its publication possible. My sense of gratitude to Ihab Hassan, Sacvan Bercovitch, and Robert Sklar is enormous. They each gave generously of their time to comment brilliantly and carefully on my work. Since their own work and writings have had a special influence upon me, I especially appreciate their help and the extent to which I have benefited from their genius and generosity.

In addition, I am also fortunate in having received considerable support from my colleagues at the University of New Mexico. I cannot exaggerate the significance to me and to this work of the encouragement and friendship of my colleagues in American studies—George Arms, Hamlin Hill, and Joel Jones. Throughout my work on this manuscript, and on other efforts as well, they have each provided me with the benefit of their experience and ideas to such a degree that their combined contribution is incalculable. Similarly, I must also thank other colleagues at the University of New Mexico in the fields of American studies and American literary scholarship who have read different sections of the book and have provided advice and help, including Peter White, James Barbour, Robert Fleming, and Ernest Baughman. Together with their colleagues in history, the arts, and the social sciences, such as Harold Rhodes and Peter Lupsha, they constitute a community of scholars that encourage, nurture, and sustain efforts toward meaningful learning and scholarship. In addition, during his semester-long visit to New Mexico, John Cawelti could not have been a better friend and adviser. After generously offering to read the manuscript, he spent much time with me in conversations about the book and about other matters related to ideas and work of mutual interest. For such a brief visit, he had an enormous impact on many of my colleagues and graduate students, who benefited from his brilliance and warm generosity. I also wish to express my appreciation to other scholars who have read either all or significant parts of this work and have provided me with the benefit of both their constructive criticism and their positive encouragement, including Alan Trachtenberg, Kermit Vanderbilt, Lawrence Buell, Kenneth S. Lynn, Joe Fashing, Leonard Kriegel, and Anthony Hilfer.

I am pleased to say that many of the ideas and interpretations in various chapters of this book had their origins in classrooms at both the University of Alabama and the University of New Mexico. So in many ways my greatest debt and deepest thanks should go to my students. At Alabama Ginia McPhearson Allen, Trisha Black, and Eddie O'Neil, each of whom worked with me on almost a semester-by-semester basis, were perhaps most representative of students from all over the state whose combination of affection and enthusiasm—along with a genuine appreciation for learning—made me feel privileged to work with them. It would, of course, be impossible to name all these students, but at the same time failing to mention at least some of those who worked most closely with me, primarily as majors in American studies courses, would make me seem uncaring about an experience of great professional and personal importance. I believe that with these students—Liz Terrell, Ginny Kilpatrick, Bill "Caffey" Norman, Cindy Lyle, Cathy Hyman Mosteller, "Hoke" Perkins, Boozer Downs, John and Molly Plunk, Sally Shields Green, Xan Foerer, Katherine and John Sullivan, Joe Hornsby, Cindy McMillan, Jennifer Burry, Charley Gaston—we created a genuine atmosphere for learning and growth that exceeded the limits of classroom walls and extended into our lives. I will always be grateful for my experiences with them as a teacher and adviser. In addition, of the many exceptional and talented graduate and undergraduate students at the University of New Mexico, I especially want to mention Jerry Henderson and Sharon Clark, among so many others, for their truly helpful, enthusiastic, and important dialogue with me in classes, seminars, and private discussions on ideas and matters directly related to this work. Again, such a list of necessity can include only those with whom I have worked most consistently and repeatedly, such as Ed Mahoney, Harriet Bloom, Rich Wilson, Ruth Banes, Kyle Fiore, Bob Michael, Cathy Bledsoe, Ron Reichel, Floyce Alexander, Bill Tydeman, J'eral Rainwater, Lola Barb, Mara Brett, Gwen Wilemon, Janie Jones, and Dave Kammer.

Earlier versions of many of the chapters in this book appeared in *American Quarterly, Studies in Short Fiction, The Centennial Review, the Midwest Quarterly, Research Studies,* and *Arizona Quarterly.* I wish to thank the editors of these journals. However, I am also especially grateful to several members of the editorial staff at the University of Texas Press: Iris Tillman Hill, Suzanne Comer, and Holly Carver. They have demonstrated sensitivity, intelligence, and creativity and have helped me learn new things about my own book and work.

Finally, I have the impossible task of trying to express through acknowledgment the most important source of help for me and this book—my family. Few who enter this profession quite realize how much others under the pressures and realities of modern academic life will have to contribute in many different ways. In a very real sense, parts of this work have been a family effort. My two oldest daughters, Katya and Meighan, made a true contribution for children their age of repeatedly helping me check quotations from such sources as Hegel, Sartre, and Isaiah Berlin. Armed with such weighty knowledge, they were able to convince to some extent the youngest, Jennifer, that the sacrifice of many weekends of hiking and roaming in the mountains of New Mexico and southern Colorado was necessary and justified for the completion of the book. My mother, of course, has been waiting for this book since before I even thought of it. Her presence during these years has not only made our lives richer and better but has also given my children an invaluable example of courage and dignity. The contribution of my wife, Scottie, involves far more than can be described here. She read and reread the manuscript in several versions and stages of development, with the only compensation being the belief that with each reading she was nearing the last time. She has made comments and suggestions that have contributed in significant ways toward its improvement. Perhaps in this context it is worth noting that among many of my friends the great crisis often seems to come in trying to find some sense of harmony between one's work and the rest of one's life. My greatest fortune is in being part of a family that makes such a harmony possible and that puts into practice what Thoreau saw as an ideal for all people: making one's "living by loving."

✌ The Law of the Heart

⚘ Chapter 1

The modern tradition and the American self: Individualism and the perverted self

In the past several decades many literary critics and historians have tended to discuss the idea of an American self or identity in terms that originate in a basically European tradition of literary modernism. While terms like "literary modernism" and "the modern tradition" defy final definition, most critics agree that, in Irving Howe's phrase, "the idea of the modern" involves more than mere chronology. "In the past hundred years," writes Howe, "we have had a special kind of literature. We call it modern and distinguish it from the merely contemporary; for where the contemporary refers to time, the modern refers to sensibility and style, and where the contemporary is a term of neutral reference, the modern is a term of critical placement and judgment."[1] Similarly, Richard Ellmann and Charles Feidelson, Jr., see the modern as referring to more than contemporaneity. "The term," according to Ellmann and Feidelson, "designates a distinctive kind of imagination—themes and forms, conditions and modes of creation, that are interrelated and comprise an imaginative whole."[2] Thus, while the most imaginative and influential critics of this movement, such as Lionel Trilling, take largely divergent and individualistic approaches to the study of the modern, we can think of a "modern" tradition or movement because of its clear association with a recognizable body of writers and thinkers whose works and ideas help shape the way we define and understand the human condition and human experience today. Moreover, among the "themes and forms" that help define this as a tradition is a "distinctive" way of thinking and writing about the idea of the self and its relationship to culture. From this aspect of the tradition we have learned to talk about the self through a vocabulary of terms—such as sincerity, consciousness, anxiety, guilt, choice, alienation, and despair—that derive from the works of major thinkers of the past two centuries. These include Blake, Hegel, and Rousseau at the historical origins of the movement up through such proponents of the supremacy of artistic consciousness as Flaubert, to the existentialism and phenomenology of Nietzsche, Kierkegaard, and Heidegger, to the writings of Freud and Marx and the concern for freedom and choice of Sartre and Jaspers. It would also be legitimate, I think, to include the contributions of more contemporary writers and thinkers, such as Herbert Marcuse, R. D. Laing, Norman O. Brown, Erik H. Erikson, and Marshall McLuhan, who further the intellectual tradition of modernism in its post–World War Two phase.

This language of the self as formed in the tradition of modernism has been used not only to analyze but also—to some extent— even to redefine the concept of an American self and an American character. For example, the method of applying the modern tradition to the study of the self while seeing the self in the very terms of the tradition underlies Ihab Hassan's study of "radical innocence" in America. Hassan states that "the paradox of American literature in our time is that to the extent it has become a unique expression of American life, it has also engaged the most vital issues Europe confronts." He goes on to maintain that "no methodology of American Studies can afford to ignore" this relationship between "modern" European and American experience. "It may have been possible to distinguish clearly between Europe and America in the time of Whitman and Emerson," he writes. "Today we lack the confidence such clarity requires."[3] Similarly, we can use this language of the modern tradition that has become so much a part of our experience to better understand not only the culture of our own time but our cultural history as well. The elements of literary modernism can be devised into a sort of bridge between past and present to provide a sense of continuity, comparison, and contrast as we search out what Hassan calls the "American form" of the "dominant image of the modern self."[4]

However, modernism involves more than simply seeing the American self in European terms or applying a European intellectual tradition to the character and culture of America. The language and vocabulary of literary modernism, with its concern for freedom, self, and culture, provide an invaluable method with which to understand these themes as they develop within American experience and thought. Moreover, to some extent modernism—through its articulation of these themes—actually serves to revivify within an American context the concepts of freedom, individualism, and the self by giving them a basis for discussion in modern experience.

In relying upon the perspectives of criticism and modernity we use what Paul de Man describes as modes of thought and investigation whose authenticity depends upon their own self-derision. De Man's recent studies render new understanding of the meaning of modernism and its potential as a means for discussing literature, history, and culture. For de Man both modernity and criticism are paradoxical concepts that exist by virtue of realizing and understanding their own impossibility. Criticism, he says, exists in crisis because it can never achieve a real or an ultimate union with its subject, while modernity must always fight and oppose one of the forces upon which it depends for its existence, namely history. De Man writes that "the notion of crisis and that of criticism are very closely linked, so much so that one could state that all true criticism occurs in the mode of crisis. To speak of a crisis of criticism is then, to some degree, redundant."[5] De Man nevertheless relates this crisis of criticism and literature to the existential crisis of the self. Fictions, he maintains, provide no answer or conclusion but only a process for continuing discovery and challenge. He writes that "the human self has experienced the void within itself and the invented fiction, far from filling the void, asserts itself as pure nothingness, *our* nothingness stated and restated by a subject that is the agent of its own instability."[6]

De Man also finds "an inherent contradiction between modernity, which is a way of acting and behaving" and the concept of historical analysis in both literature and culture. For him "the authentic spirit of modernity" is captured in "Nietzsche's ruthless forgetting, the blindness with which he throws himself into an action lightened of all previous experience." According to this definition all literature, in its hope of achieving immediacy and total intimacy, becomes modern. Of course, this very process of attempting to escape history creates its own history. Nietzsche discovers that history and modernity must ultimately transcend their own opposition because of their mutual dependence upon each other.[7]

In the process of this discovery we also find that the double paradox of the redundancy of criticism and crisis and the opposition of modernity and history presents us with a further argument for using a critical methodology based on modernity for the study of American culture and character.[8] Both the attempt to find authentic selfhood and the attempt to override and escape the chains of history are concepts intrinsic to the American experience. In de Man's terms America has been a modern culture since its inception. Authenticity and immediacy in the modernist sense are basic concepts and values that go back to the very origins of our history and to the roots of our culture and character. We have fought the past and history in order to preserve as a culture our power to create and determine our freedom of the moment and our hopes for an open future. In this sense the American mind anticipated Nietzsche's dreadful experience of the impossibility of facing one's future without also confronting one's past and present.

Accordingly, the following study uses the modernist mode to discuss the American self. In the writings and ideas of significant figures in our literature and culture, modernism helps us discern different patterns of presenting the self within American thought and experience. These patterns indicate a tension between a humanistic and pragmatic conception of democratic individualism that confronts and reconciles itself to the paradox of history and modernity as opposed to a defensive image of the self that retreats within itself. In such figures as Cooper, Poe, and Charles Ives we get a turning inward away from pragmatic experience, autonomy, and history toward an inner self that achieves a false security for itself, its ideals, its vision of truth and hope. The "inner" self feels free and secure through its sense of transcendence of the dangers, questions, uncertainties, turmoils, and demands of ordinary experience. However, in other writers the idea of the self and freedom relate in a more complex way to reality and culture. Such writers as Emerson, Whitman, and Henry James tend to incorporate in their language and ideas the cultural dialogue between democratic as opposed to totalitarian versions of the individual self. On the whole, these particular writers—along with Howells, William James, Fitzgerald, and Dewey, among others—assimilate within their thought and works proclivities toward totalitarian or "imperial" models of the self in a way that enables them to articulate and promulgate a very different tradition of democratic individualism. In these writers we get highly original attempts to present a self that relates a sense of its own autonomy and individuality to the mutability of reality. Thus, some of these figures can be studied as proposing at different times and with varying degrees of self-consciousness programs for the development of confidence in the concept of individualism in a democratic culture. Such programs generally tend to relate basic American myths of a transcendent self and an Edenic landscape to more pragmatic and humanistic approaches to the fundamental issues of achieving selfhood and identity within American culture. By definition such programs cannot be absolute or final. However, they are more than just casual responses to the modern crisis of the self. Their commitment to individuality and freedom reflects concepts of culture and of reality as open, pluralistic, and changing. In general their discussions and presentations of these issues are in the tradition delineated by Whitman and William James in which the world of myth and the ideal interacts in important and complicated ways with the real and the empirical. The growth of the mass culture over the past century makes the establishment of such relationships between the ideal and the real even more important.

Moreover, since the middle of the nineteenth century major economic and social changes in America have undermined the traditional basis for theories of the autonomous self and the freedom of the individual. Changes involving the rise of an urban proletariat and a mercenary plutocracy, the loss of the belief in progress—which came to be seen as an illusion no longer consistent with American realities—the decline in traditional religious belief, the collapse of a sense of either community or social order, the growing contrast between work and leisure, the fragmentation of culture itself in accordance with social, religious, and economic interests and prejudices all helped attenuate the traditional sense of the integrity of the individual self. This background of change served to exacerbate the confusion and distortion in American culture between individual freedom in the pragmatic sense as opposed to transcendence in the sense of escape. The transcendent American became isolated from the very conditions and culture that gave the American a sense of self and identity. In the past several decades, however, literary modernism has provided a new context within which to revivify the debate over the nature of the American self.

The modernist approach to the literature and culture of America nurtures critical controversy and debate. Modernist critics of American culture differ widely in their interpretations. For instance, Frederick J. Hoffman gives us an interesting example of the use of the language of modernity to describe the inward turn of the American self upon itself. More pessimistic than Hassan, he perceives a modern self that is forced "to preserve the self" in a situation involving "the retreat of the ego, its withdrawal inward, into a state of fear and self-analysis."[9] Hoffman's sense of the origins of the American self helps explain his pessimism. He sees the modern self as a reaction to the end of the open space of the unsettled wilderness that cultivated the original American "exploring self." He further argues that a sort of "grammar of this experience" of space once defined American character and "the moral figure of the self" in America. "The power of space over the conscience lasts only so long as space is available," he writes. "But its influence on the imagination also depends upon its actual qualities. The American Adam, forever shifting the locale of his Eden, eventually encountered a Hell."[10] Richard Poirier, on the other hand, evaluates this inward turn of the American mind and self in a way that diverges sharply from Hoffman's view. Poirier sees such an inward turn as involving an artistic act of the American imagination that fosters creativity and originality and creates, in his phrase, "a world elsewhere" that constitutes not a retreat from but a reinvention of reality. He argues that "a modernistic impulse" in American fiction and culture places the priority not upon the physical environment that Hoffman sees as so influential in developing an expansive sense of self but upon "an environment in language" for the creation of "an environment of 'freedom.'" Poirier further sees that in some ways the openness of the American environment could have had a stultifying effect upon the self. To preserve the self in such a vastness required an exercise of imagination and consciousness, a sort of "visionary possession of landscape" that could weaken and diminish the self through overextension.[11] Thus, while modernism for a critic like Hoffman seems to constitute in both critical and social dimensions the diminution and disintegration of the self, for Poirier the same tradition becomes a way of presenting and elaborating upon what he later calls "a performing self," a creative individual self which functions as a manifestation of the American writer's visionary attitude toward language and the imagination.

Furthermore, Poirier's emphasis on the free and creative imagination represents a modernist version of the Puritan vision, as Sacvan Bercovitch interprets it, "of the American paradise as the fulfillment of scripture prophecy." Poirier's thesis of a free environment of language relates to the Puritan vision of the self and the landscape. Bercovitch writes that "the American made his sainthood visible by identifying the literal-spiritual contours of the land." He further states that primarily in the Puritan vision of the landscape "is the Puritan concept of intermediate identity more strongly affirmed—where intermediacy, we recall, indicates not a historical limitation but a comprehensive prophetic self-hood."[12] Similarly, Poirier interprets the vision of the landscape by the creative American imagination as a projection onto the landscape of the artistic self. In the same way in which the Puritans read the landscape in terms of their own self-fulfilling prophecy, the American writers, according to Poirier, saw in the landscape the fulfillment of their artistic consciousness and imagination that would bring light and meaning to that landscape.[13] Equally interesting is the way in which modernism can support a tradition of democracy and democratic culture that ironically at times seemed to be its intellectual contradiction and its enemy. The roots of the modern tradition in early and middle nineteenth-century Europe can be found to a considerable extent in the opposition of an intellectual and cultural elite to the rise of democracy in both Europe and America. Both Kierkegaard and Nietzsche saw their individualism as opposing the growing power of the masses. Moreover, if we relate modernism to Dwight Macdonald's idea of the avant-garde, the original gap between the modern tradition and democratic culture seems even more profound. Macdonald describes avant-garde as "the movement from which most of the enduring work of our time has come," partly through its separation from and its "systematic opposition" to the rise of the masses. According to Macdonald, "the old avant-garde of 1870–1930 from Rimbaud to Picasso" was composed of "a peculiar mixture of conservatism and revolutionism," with people who became "an elite community, a rather snobbish one," but one that still was open to individual effort and creativity.[14] Macdonald ends his essay with a lengthy quotation from Kierkegaard as a summary of his own attack on mass culture. The difference, therefore, between what we think of as democratic culture and the modern tradition seems even more profound than the contradictions within democratic culture itself between elitism and egalitarianism.[15]

It therefore comes as a great irony to find that the same democratic tradition which viewed the modernist obsession with art and elitism in Europe with such suspicion turns to modernism to develop a new basis for discussing the concepts of individualism and autonomy that are traditional factors in American democratic thought. The vocabulary of the self in modernism carries over into the mid twentieth century and becomes for many a basic component for any modern theory of freedom and the individual self. Thus, David Riesman offers an interesting example of the use of the language of the modern tradition to discuss and analyze democratic culture. "The very fluidity of modern democratic social systems," he writes, "that, for the mass of people results in anxiety and 'escape from freedom,' forces those who would become autonomous to find their own way. They must 'choose themselves,' in Sartre's phrase, out of their very alienation from traditional ties and inner-directed defenses which inhibited true choice in the past. However, I think Sartre is mistaken in his Kantian notion that men can choose themselves under total-itarian conditions. If most of the choices that matter are made for us by the social system, even if it is in appearance a democratic system, then our sense of freedom also will atrophy: most people need the opportunity for some freedom of behavior if they are to develop and confirm their autonomy of character."[16] Riesman's language indicates the tendency to use terms derived from mod-ernism to reformulate old definitions of individualism and auton-omy and to reconsider basic questions about the strength of the foundation for freedom and democratic culture in today's world.

Accordingly, Louis Hartz sees Riesman along with Erich Fromm, certainly representative of much in the modern tradition, as avatars of a "new individualism" in America. "The twentieth century," writes Hartz, "has witnessed the emergence of a new kind of American individualism, the individualism of non-conform-ity, which actually challenges the compulsive democracy of the Lockean individualism by which the nation has centrally and his-torically lived. The new individualism has arisen curiously, with-out our quite observing it. In part this is because we have needed the decade of the fifties, of the very recent past, to make it into a genuine tradition of modern American thought. Surely the work of writers like Fromm, Riesman, and Whyte, the whole assault on conformity which followed the decline of McCarthy, is basic to any evaluation of this trend."[17]

Proponents of this "modern" version of individualism, with its basis in both traditional democratic culture and "the modern tradition," see it as a meaningful alternative to several different kinds of attacks upon the viability and significance of democratic individualism in the contemporary world. Besides providing a coherent system of thought from which to counter Theodore

Dreiser's naturalistic argument for "an end to all thought of individuality,"[18] the "new individualism," as Hartz describes it, offers an alternative to what Hoffman says are arguments for individualism based on "dogmatic innocence"—"desperate assertions of the 'dogma' of the self against what appear to be overwhelming evidences denying its autonomy."[19] A meaningful theory of democratic individualism must also deal with another version of the individual self as "dogmatic innocence" in the form of what Quentin Anderson sees as the "imperial self." Anderson maintains that the emphasis on an Emersonian inner self in American culture—a version also one could argue of Hassan's "radical innocence" as well as Hoffman's "dogmatic innocence"—represents a secularization of the Puritan religious impulse. As a leading spokesman for this movement Emerson, according to Anderson, "was taking the only step available to him to save what he thought essential in religion. There was no temple for the god save the self." Anderson sees this elevation of the self as a radical departure from the language and ideas of both Jefferson and the authors of the *Federalist* papers.[20] Thus, it becomes a significant perversion of individualism in American culture.

While Anderson's Eriksonian theory of the origins of the imperial self in the psychological conflict between the Transcendentalists and earlier generations over identity helps account for the Emersonian concern for selfhood and reality, we also need to remember that many of the Transcendentalists saw themselves as carrying forward in their own time and in their own way the moral and cultural obligations inherited from their Puritan and revolutionary era ancestors. It is this sort of continuity from Edwards to Emerson that Bercovitch emphasizes in his study of the development of the idea of an American self and identity. For Emerson, according to Bercovitch, history became meaningful "only when he turned to America."[21] Thus, continuity and tradition along with rebellion played their role in the development of the American self.

The discussion so far involves literary modernism and the American self to determine a proclivity in American literature and culture either toward versions of a so-called "new individualism" or toward an "imperial" or "dogmatic" sense of an isolated self. At this point, however, it becomes necessary to place these images of the modern American self in another context. Whether seen as an imperious and dogmatic self or as a continuity of a democratic tradition of freedom, Emerson's program for individual selfhood needs to be examined within the context of the attempt of the modern mind to find a basis in political theory for individualism consistent with modern consciousness and experience. Emerson and those who followed him faced the same dilemma of adumbrating in modern terms a meaningful foundation upon which to build a concept of an independent and autonomous political self. Like John Stuart Mill, the American Transcendentalists were caught between the inadequacies of the two conventional arguments on behalf of individual liberty—the "natural rights theory of the civil liberties" and the theory of individualism based on "freedom's social utility." As Albert William Levi writes, "The classical mode of the justification of individual liberty is the doctrine of natural rights. Guaranteed by God, or inherent in the order of Nature, these rights are absolute, inalienable, and self-evident. But Mill specifically abandons a natural rights theory of the civil liberties in favor of the doctrine that they are a public utility. . . . And in so doing, in suggesting that the values of freedom are primarily social values, he opens the way for society itself to be the judge of freedom's social utility. But if the judgment of the social value of freedom is left to that type of democratic choice in which the authority resides in a majority of those whose interests are at stake . . . then just this (ironically enough) is to invite that very tyranny of the majority against which the essay *On Liberty* was specifically directed."[22]

A proposed solution for Mill's paradox of the nature and foundation of liberty involves what Levi terms "a self-realizational theory of civil liberties."[23] However, this proposed solution does not get us out of the dilemma of modern liberty that Mill and others faced. In fact, it really opens another level of discussion involving selfhood and the nature of liberty that perhaps even more closely relates to the dilemma Emerson faced in his program of American selfhood. In his presentation of a fictional self in the form of the poet or the scholar who is capable of bringing all Americans a sense of individualism and freedom derived from their common connection to a mythic American self, Emerson in effect became involved in what Isaiah Berlin considers to be a vital and basic distinction within the concept of individual liberty—"the negative liberty of non-interference" as opposed to "the positive liberty of self-realization."[24] Put simply, negative freedom concerns freedom from interference by external forces that can limit the action of the individual. Negative liberty basically proclaims the existence of a recognizable frontier between the powers of the individual and the infringement of the state or community. Positive liberty, on the other hand, tends to emphasize and deal with the realization of an "ideal" or "higher" or "real" self "not so much in individual men," says Berlin, "as incarnated in institutions, traditions, forms of life wider than the empirical spatio-temporal existence of the finite individual."[25]

Berlin emphasizes that both concepts of liberty, which at different times can function together and balance each other, are subject to their own forms of perversion. The negative liberty of noninterference, as Mill sometimes failed to see, can perpetuate social evil and injustice while contributing to the lack of freedom for others. Berlin, however, feels that in the modern world the greater danger to freedom lies in the perversion of the positive form of liberty. He says, "Each concept seems liable to perversion into the very vice which it was created to resist. But whereas liberal ultra-individualism could scarcely be said to be a rising force at present, the rhetoric of 'positive' liberty, at least in its distorted form, is in far greater evidence, and continues to play its historical role (in both capitalist and anti-capitalist societies) as a cloak for despotism in the name of a wider freedom."[26]

Berlin fears that positive liberty easily becomes a license to violate the rights of others in the name of the "higher" or "real" self from which its authority and power come. The great irony for this concept of freedom in its perverted form is that the search for a "higher" or "true" self, rather than leading to a sense of expansion and involvement, can become, in Berlin's phrase, "a strategic retreat into an inner citadel" of the self for protection. This is a form of freedom Berlin dreads. He says, "All political isolationism, all economic autarky, every form of autonomy, has in it some element of this attitude. I eliminate the obstacles in my path by abandoning the path; I retreat into my own sect, my own planned economy, my own deliberated insulated territory, where no voices from outside need be listened to, and no external forces can have effect. This is a form of the search for security; but it has also been called the search for personal or national freedom or independence."[27]

The different images of an American self as forms of dogmatic innocence or an imperial self are American versions of what Berlin calls positive liberty. It seems to me that both Hoffman and Anderson interpret the Emersonian defense of individual freedom and the self in America during the nineteenth century as a perverted form of positive liberty. A significant model of the effort to explain freedom in terms of a "higher" self can be found in Hegel's description, in *The Phenomenology of Mind*, of "the Law of the Heart." In this discussion, Hegel expatiates upon the psychology of a situation of increasing estrangement between idealism and intractable reality. This tension enables one to infuse personal needs and wishes with a sense of universal significance and moral righteousness. "In its new attitude," Hegel writes, "self-consciousness regards itself as the necessary element. It knows that it has the universal, the law, immediately within itself, a law which, because of this characteristic of being immediately within consciousness as it is for itself, is called the Law of the *Heart*." This law, which stands for "self-consciousness" or "the heart," at first appears to be some sort of liberator against a seemingly dehumanizing and oppressive reality. "Opposed to this 'heart' stands a reality," writes Hegel. "This reality," he continues, "is thus on the one hand a law by which the particular individuality is crushed and oppressed, a violent ordinance of the world which contradicts the law of the heart, and, on the other hand, a humanity suffering under that ordinance—a humanity which does not follow the law of the heart, but is subjected to an alien necessity." Through estranging itself and realizing itself, the law of the heart achieves actuality and ceases to be the law of the heart. "The individual," as Hegel says, "in establishing his own ordinance, no longer finds it to be his own."[28]

Thus, the law of the heart and the individual through that law continually defeat themselves. "The law of 'this individual heart' is alone that wherein self-consciousness recognizes itself; but the universal and accepted ordinance has by actualizing that law become for self-consciousness likewise its own essential nature and its own reality." The perverseness, the resulting madness, describes the continuing frustration of the self as its law of the heart meets perennial destruction by "its own reality." Hegel writes: "In that it gives expression to this moment of its own conscious destruction, and thereby expresses the result of its experience, it shows itself to be this inner perversion of itself, to be consciousness gone crazy, its own essence being immediately not essence, its reality immediately unreality."[29] Thus, according to Ernst Cassirer's interpretation and understanding of this principle of the heart, the individual in learning of the inability to impose the law of the heart upon the actual world realizes that this law "becomes a destructive and subversive principle." In attempting to enforce the law, the individual realizes the strength of the resistance mounted against it. Such resistance, says Cassirer, can ultimately be circumvented only by "abrogating the whole historical order of things."[30]

In America the law of the heart as a form of the perversion of positive liberty became a cultural force not because of Emerson, who scorned isolation and the separation of thought from the active self, but at least in part because of the vacuum created by the distortion of the liberal tradition and its basic tenets. Personal liberty and independence exist today in a way that the founders and speakers for the liberal tradition never intended. Jefferson, for example, made an important distinction between "rightful liberty" as the "unobstructed action according to our will within limits drawn around us by the equal rights of others" and an odious form of liberty that involved simply "unobstructed action according to our will."[31] "Every man," Jefferson maintained, "is under the natural duty of contributing to the necessities of the society and this is all the law should enforce on him."[32] Thus, the Jefferson who so strongly espoused continuous rebellion in the service of liberty saw the inseparability of private and public liberty. He anticipated that the failure to relate personal action and liberty to social and political institutions would cultivate slavery. In calling "lethargy the forerunner of death to the public liberty," he agreed with Madison in seeing self-interest and liberty as factors that are interrelated with the need in a democratic culture for an operational system of mutually dependent factions.[33] Jefferson and Madison shared a dread of society in which people live independently of each other, because this kind of freedom serves as a mask for the breakdown of both individual personality and free institutions. Madison especially feared the introduction into the government of "a will independent of the society itself." He wanted to cultivate counteraction between conflicting sets of ambitions and interests so that "each may be a check on the other—that the private interest of every individual may be a sentinel over the public rights."[34] While independence today often connotes separation, the Federalists and Jeffersonians saw themselves as living in dependence upon other groups and other people. The condition of interdependence and mutual dependence would endue each citizen with a sense of personal, political, and social responsibility.

For them a society based on no dependence between groups or people would result in some form of anarchy or tyranny. Politically, it would mean disaster. Psychologically, it would mean a condition of alienation for all people.

Unfortunately, however, it is independence in this sense of isolation that has survived today in spite of efforts by such thinkers as Veblen, Howells, William James, and Dewey to formulate a new definition of individualism to correspond with new political, social, and economic realities. For Dewey the perversion of the liberal conception of personal liberty into a popularized notion of independence served the trend toward massification by undermining true individualism. He argued that isolation and insecurity were the illegitimate offspring of an unwholesome union between democracy and big business.[35] However, one can also see this situation as an outgrowth of another aspect of the nature of freedom in America. The wilderness and frontier experience in this country contributed to the rise of the law of the heart as a cultural and political force. Irving Howe has discussed this theme in our culture, especially as it manifests itself in literature, in terms of "anarchy" as opposed to "authority." He argues that in the writings of James Fenimore Cooper the "anarchist vision . . . first appears with imaginative strength."[36] While I agree completely with Howe, it is also possible to see this anarchist vision both psychologically and metaphysically in terms of Hegel's law of the heart in the sense of the individual's fight with the realities of both civilization and the wilderness. Certainly Cooper offers psychological insights into American culture for many critics who see in the Leatherstocking novels several different patterns of movement whose meaning can best be understood as a simulacrum of deeper patterns in the American psyche. There is, for example, the double meaning, as John William Ward so clearly states, of the movement from the East to the West, with its conflicting images of the East and Europe as embodying all that is valuable in culture and of the West as symbolic of nature, the wilderness, and freedom.[37] There is the movement in the direction of perennial youth—"a gradual sloughing of the old skin, towards a new youth," as Lawrence says. "It is the myth of America." But there is also another aspect in Cooper of this myth of America that Lawrence broadcasts. As an archetypal American hero, Natty Bumpo also becomes for Lawrence "a saint with a gun." Lawrence writes: "But you have there the myth of the essential white American. All the other stuff, the love, the democracy, the floundering into lust, is a sort of by-play. The essential American soul is hard, isolate, stoic, and a killer. It has never yet melted." It is this aspect of Lawrence's understanding of the myth as the "story of the collapse of the white psyche" and of the American white "divided against himself" that most pertains to an understanding of Cooper in terms of the conflict of the law of the heart with reality.[38]

In one of the earlier novels in the Leatherstocking series, *The Prairie*, the focus stays on the tension between the conflicting values of wilderness and law, individual and society.[39] However, the final novel of the series, *The Deerslayer*, returns Natty to his youth while giving the law of the heart special emphasis, elevation, and dignity. The novel continues the usual Cooper themes of cultural contradiction, but the focus shifts to what I consider to be Natty's perverted sense of freedom founded on moral superiority and independence. In an early conversation with Hurry Harry about the authority of whites in taking Indian scalps, Deerslayer demonstrates his understanding of the gap between his own conception of moral issues and reality. "I do not pretend," he says, "that all that white men do is properly Christianized, and according to the lights given them, for then they would be what they *ought* to be, which we know they are not."[40] He then proceeds to describe for Hurry Harry a sort of hierarchy of values, ending with God's laws, to which a final personal appeal is possible. "When the Colony's laws, or even the King's laws, run ag'in the laws of God, they get to be onlawful, and ought not to be obeyed. I hold to a white man's respecting white laws, so long as they do not cross the track of a law comin' from a higher authority.... But 'tis useless talking, as each man will think for himself, and have his say agreeable to his thoughts" (p. 36).

Toward the middle of the novel Cooper, as though no longer able to contain himself, directly addresses the reader about Natty's superior qualities, based on his access to an "Infinite Source" which imbues him with a "moral sense" and a "steadiness that no danger could appall or any crisis disturb" (p. 276). In accordance with this moral superiority, Deerslayer's individuality triumphs over history. However, such freedom demands a tragic sacrifice of an important part of himself and of his capacity for human experience. Deerslayer proves incapable of accepting Judith Hutter's love because such love in and of itself would contaminate his freedom and independence. Also, Judith's past history does not conform to his conception of morality. Her reality is unacceptable so, in a sense, he destroys it. In his inability to love and feel we see the perversity of his heart's victory and the cost to the self of the triumph of the individual consciousness—Hegel's law of the heart.

At the end of the book Deerslayer returns to the scene of the novel's events after a fifteen-year absence. In rummaging around the remains of his former life, he finds a trace of the rejected woman. "The heart of Deerslayer beat quick as he found a ribbon of Judith's fluttering from a log," writes Cooper (p. 563). The ribbon, Cooper admits, "recalled all her beauty." But the emotion never achieves completion, as Cooper asserts: "... and, we may add, all her failings." Cooper then adds: "Although the girl had never touched his heart, the Hawkeye, for so we ought now to call him, still retained a kind and sincere interest in her welfare." The bearer now of still another name indicating even greater forest feats, Hawkeye clearly has removed himself from common human experience in order to preserve the freedom of his heart and his inner consciousness. The irrelevance and inadequacy of his kindness and sincerity seem clear in the sentence that follows, with its ironic suggestion of lost possibilities and hopes. "He tore away the ribbon," writes Cooper, "and knotted it to the stock of Killdeer, which had been the gift of the girl herself" (p. 563).

To R. W. B. Lewis Deerslayer represents a form of symbolic, mythic hero, the American Adam, who appears in different guises in the writings of not only Cooper but Thoreau, Melville, Hawthorne, Fitzgerald, Faulkner, and others. "Natty Bumpo," writes Lewis, "is the full-fledged fictional Adam." Like Isaac McCaslin in Faulkner's *The Bear*, Deerslayer witnesses his own "rebirth as the American Adam: accomplished appropriately in the forest on the edge of a lake, with no parents near at hand, no sponsors at the baptism; springing from nowhere, as Tocqueville had said, standing alone in the presence of God and Nature." In addition to his capacity to renew his innocence through such rebirth, Deerslayer successfully fulfills his role as the American Adam through other special qualities of moral independence and superiority that distinguish him from ordinary mortals. Lewis writes that "as Hawkeye becomes secure in his characteristic virtues" he completes his rise to the status of Adamic hero "largely by opposition to the habits of the others around him. Less important than the melodrama of the capture and rescue of Hurry Harry and Tom Hutter is Hawkeye's growing awareness that, while they fight and collect scalps for profit, his own 'gifts' require him to come to terms with his forest home, to kill solely in order to live there."[41] The centrality of this archetypal American hero, who symbolizes and turns into myth the major ambiguities of our culture concerning freedom and culture and the individual and society, seems natural. However, the implications and significance of this archetypal American hero for our understanding of freedom in America become clearer through a comparison of him to the symbolic conception of the modern individual, who seems to a writer like Georg Lukács to be alienated and victimized by freedom.

For Lukács modernism includes none of the promise for freedom and the self that others have seen in the tradition. In fact he takes to an extreme the feeling and fear of writers we discussed earlier, who see in modernism only a dehumanizing and self-destructive movement. Thus, at face value Lewis in *The American Adam* and Lukács in "The Ideology of Modernism" describe types or characters who seem to be in total opposition. Moreover, this opposition stems partly from the fact that Lewis and Lukács develop mythic types who are symbolic of different centuries and cultures. Lewis, of course, in his study of the Adamic myth, delineates what was seen as a hope and a possibility for people in the agrarian and bucolic, the open and free atmosphere of nineteenth-century America. Lukács in contrast deals with a constricting environment that had already turned into a living nightmare. When Lewis celebrates the aspects of American culture that can produce what he considers to be a superior character type, he recalls a vision of an environment capable of at least promising to give each person an opportunity to create a unique and individual identity in a truly democratic fashion and in a manner idealized by such as Thoreau and Whitman. He describes a myth that was seen as giving each individual a workable possibility. The ideal as some of our most representative writers understood it was actually within the realm of possibility in the new garden of America. In addition, not only the conditions of the environment but the political system and cultural values were consistent with the myth. In contrast, Lukács deals with a world which many felt crippled the individual. While Lewis honors writers who advance a myth of freedom and creativity that encourages individual autonomy and cultural identity, Lukács of course believes the writers in the subjectivist modern tradition perpetuate and even help create the very conditions they despise. For Lukács the modern individual as depicted in modernist literature can only retreat inward.

Thus, with all these clear and important differences it is interesting to find that similarities emerge in the description of these

mobility. Yet the mythology and the value system it supported remained even after the objective conditions that had justified it had vanished. We have, I think, continued to associate democracy and progress with perpetual social mobility (both horizontal and vertical) and with the continual expansion of our power into new fields or new levels of exploitation. Under the aspect of this myth, our economic, social, and spiritual life is taken to be a series of initiations, of stages in a movement outward and upward toward some transcendent goal."[47]

Such criticism encourages some concern about the strength of the foundations upon which the Adamic hero's freedom rests. It suggests a basic fallibility and speciousness in the nature of the freedom and the quality of the character that the Adamic hero symbolizes. In a garden which he inherited, the American Adam's world was based so thoroughly upon his personal proclivities that it inevitably turned from a dream of paradise into a nightmare of emotional and psychological deprivations. The myth shows in all its power and promise the total commitment in the American mind to personal freedom at the same time that it indicates its greatest failure and weakness in the form of its inability to find the means for protecting and preserving such freedom. Based in part, as Slotkin indicates, on exclusionary attitudes toward women and non-Anglo-Saxons, the myth contains its own destruction in the form of its very reliance upon an isolated self unable to enter into meaningful and creative social relationships. The American Adam's conception of freedom disengages the individual in a manner that makes ultimate isolation, the attenuation of the self, and the surrender of individuality inevitable. When applied to this central myth of American culture, Lukács' critique of modernism helps explain the Adamic myth as a form of the perverted self, of the law of the heart, operating toward its own destruction. This view of the myth reinforces Gertrude Stein's insight that America entered the twentieth century long before any other nation.

Clearly, a feeling of responsibility for finding possible alternatives to our current imbroglio influences many cultural critics and historians in forming their theories of the modern era of mass culture. However, any viable type of democracy will need to confront and overcome the tradition of the perverted self or the law of the heart and will also need to devise a synthesis of modernism and liberal democracy that emphasizes the individual's interdependent relationship with the community. Moreover, in today's post-Marxian, post-Freudian world, yesterday's unfashionable ideas and thinkers that once seemed remote from modern concerns may suddenly appear relevant and useful. For example, William James' philosophy of humanism and pluralism based on "pure experience" and individuality may provide the outline for a model from which to build a meaningful discussion of the role of the individual in contemporary democratic society. His uninhibited commitment to democratic individualism and freedom constitutes the desiderata in the writings of many current students of popular and democratic culture. Without such a commitment, we will see only the continuation of a long process of the deterioration of both culture and self. We will move from what Cassirer calls the tragedy of culture to the tragedy of pop—embodying the modernist nightmare of an intellectual, artistic, and political elite imprisoned by its dependence upon the masses with which it lives in mutual hatred, fear, and envy.

♘ Chapter 2
Poe and the transcendent self

In America "the perverted self" found its model author in the early stages of our modern literature in Edgar Allan Poe. The radical ideas of cultural, psychological, and personal transcendence that have attracted so much attention in the rebellion of the past ten years were limned in the work and mind of Poe. Of course, few critics study Poe as a writer with political content or see him in terms of any relationship to the liberal tradition. However, in a complex way Poe's modernity relates significantly to politics and to the crisis of the liberal tradition. Poe anticipates the thrust in our age to replace political statements with other cultural actions and forms. He challenges traditional liberal consciousness and values by impugning their relevance. In an inchoate stage we get in Poe an insight into the potential power of cultural forms that supersede traditional political institutions and thereby make it possible to subsume within themselves the power and authority that once went to conventional political expressions and forms. The priority Poe places upon the self and art contains a covert political message and a prophecy for traditional liberalism: its greatest challenge may come not from any other political system that at least recognizes and respects political consciousness and modes but from a force that offers an alternative in the form of artistic and cultural consciousness. Poe, therefore, helps broaden our definition and our understanding of the concept of politics.

To a degree this expanded and altered sense of politics has become a commonplace today. As Lionel Trilling says, "It is the wide sense of the word that is nowadays forced upon us, for clearly it is no longer possible to think of politics except as the politics of culture, the organization of human life toward some end or other, toward the modification of sentiments, which is to say the quality of human life." Trilling goes on to assert that in fact the liberal tradition and imagination will need to accommodate to this broader definition and can do so by honestly facing the cultural implications of the liberal political position. "The word liberal," he writes, "is a word primarily of political import, but its political meaning defines itself by the quality of life it envisages, by the sentiments it desires to affirm."[1] Insofar as these sentiments of liberalism involve a commitment to community and society—to, ironically, culture itself in the broadest sense of the term—Poe's works stand in opposition to them.[2] Poe signifies for modern culture a revolt through the form of artistic consciousness and through violently unconventional life styles and values. Thus, to a considerable extent his stories dramatize the implications for both the individual and the culture of the law of the heart and the perverted self.

Of course, without really considering or elaborating upon the political implications of their studies, many critics have discussed Poe in this way as an individual consciousness in rebellion against the dominant culture of his time. They see his tales as stories of a single mind or personality in conflict with itself and with its external environment. For example, "the typical Poe story," writes Richard Wilbur, "is, in its action, an allegory of dream experience: it occurs within the mind of a poet; the characters are not distinct personalities, but principles or faculties of the poet's divided nature."[3] Critics who have reached a similar conclusion frequently employ versions and combinations of both existential and psychoanalytical approaches, to describe the relationship of this single self to the world it inhabits in Poe's stories.[4] In their studies of Poe's works as explorations into a mind whose history symbolizes the nature of the human psyche and the anxiety of the human condition, some of these critics have compared him to such important figures as Kierkegaard, Kafka, and Otto Rank. If we add to such studies an analysis of Poe's stories in the light of R. D. Laing's work on schizophrenia, our understanding of the self and its relationships in these stories should be furthered. Moreover, Laing's model of the mind in many ways represents a modern version of the concept of the perverted self and the law of the heart. By using Laing as a means for studying Poe, we can deepen our understanding not only of how the perverted self functions in Poe but of the implications for the culture as a whole of the law of the heart.

As an existential psychiatrist, Laing provides some insights into the existential condition of many of Poe's characters in terms of their "schizoid way of being-in-the-world" as divided, disembodied, and false selves.[5] For Laing schizophrenia emerges out of ontological insecurity, a condition in which "the individual in the ordinary circumstances of living may feel more unreal than real; in a literal sense, more dead than alive; precariously differentiated from the rest of the world, so that his identity and autonomy are always in question" (*TDS*, p. 42). For such a person, according to Laing, reality itself can be the persecutor (*TDS*, p. 46). Anxiety becomes his regular mode of dealing with a world that threatens to destroy him. Such a person, says Laing, develops a special kind of relationship to himself that can be characterized as disembodiment or transcendence. In an act of "self" defense, the person dissociates what he considers to be a "transcendent" or "inner" or "disembodied" self from the rest of the body. He creates in turn a "false-self system" through which the disembodied self can deal with hostile reality. "What the individual regards as his true self," writes Laing, "is experienced as more or less disembodied and bodily experience and actions are in turn felt to be a part of the false-self system" (*TDS*, p. 78).

Laing, of course, recognizes that even basically ontologically secure persons experience this schizoid process to some degree. Using the term "schizoid" in an existential rather than a strictly clinical context, he believes that his model of the mind makes it possible to discern "a comprehensible transition from the sane schizoid way of being-in-the-world to a psychotic way of being-in-the-world" (*TDS*, p. 17). In the psychotic state the individual loses all touch with reality. "In many schizophrenics," Laing writes, "the self-body split remains the basic one. However, when the 'centre' fails to hold, neither self-experience nor body-experience can retain identity, integrity, cohesiveness, or vitality, and the individual becomes precipitated into a condition the end result of which we suggested could be described as a state of 'chaotic non-entity'" (*TDS*, p. 162). He writes that "the effort to sustain a transcendent self, out of danger and in remote control of direct experiencing and action, issues in unwished-for consequences that may far outweigh what apparent gains there seemed to be" (*TDS*, pp. 83–84). At least prior to the mystical turn of his later writings, Laing seemed to believe that the psychotic stage of schizophrenia could be described as a nightmare experience, a state of perennial shadowboxing. Unable to escape these fears, the individual fights, swinging at a false self that becomes the enemy.

Laing's approach to schizophrenia in its extreme stage affords us some insight into the operations of the psychic forces propelling characters in several Poe stories, including "The Fall of the

House of Usher." As Patrick F. Quinn says, this "story is most readily intelligible as another fable of the split personality."[6] Poe prepares the reader for this kind of interpretation in the opening lines of the story, in which we meet the narrator, a lonely traveler on a lonely road whose despondent mental state immediately reveals itself through his descriptions of the landscape and the House of Usher. In the first two lines the narrator's self-contradiction about the source of his depression further suggests that the problem rests more in his own mind than in external reality. In the second line he says that, "with the first glimpse of the building, a sense of insufferable gloom pervaded my spirit."[7] But this follows his description in the first line of a journey in which the day was "dark and soundless," the country was "dreary," and "the clouds hung oppressively low in the heavens" (p. 95). Further sustaining the impression of his unstable relationship to reality is his recollection of the journey as consuming one day—although it required traveling by horseback into a distant part of the country, which would usually require more time. As Laing writes of the ontologically insecure person: "He may lack the experience of his own temporal continuity. He may not possess an over-riding sense of personal consistency or cohesiveness" (*TDS*, p. 42).

Wilbur, who concentrates on the dreamlike quality of the characters' state of mind in this story, states that "Roderick Usher, then, is a part of the narrator's self."[8] However, Laing's existential concept of schizophrenia helps us understand that the narrator's journey also constitutes a metaphor for the separation of that self from its own body. The chronology of that process of disembodiment or transcendence certainly had begun for the narrator by the time he received the letter from Usher. This fantastic communication in itself indicated the self's feeling of danger and insecurity and its concomitant desire to assert and protect its own existence by creating a relationship with itself. "The self," writes Laing, "avoids being related directly to real persons but relates itself to itself and the objects which it itself posits. *The self can relate with immediacy to an object which is an object of its own imagination or memory but not to a real person*" (*TDS*, p. 86).

In "The Fall of the House of Usher," the nature of this relationship achieves symbolic clarity when the narrator confronts the House of Usher and its setting. On his arrival, the narrator views the house, which represents his state of mind.[9] However, in an existential sense, the house as a physical representation of the narrator's state of mind and state of being functions symbolically as his other or false self. The scene effectively illustrates the narrator's schizoid way of being-in-the-world as a disembodied self involved in a relationship with a false or other self. Furthermore, the narrator's perception of the house and its setting demonstrates a continued unconscious awareness of his situation and a prescience of the ineluctable conflict and endless splitting of the self that the process implies. "Perhaps," he says, "the eye of a scrutinizing observer might have discovered a barely perceptible fissure, which, extending from the roof of the building in front, made its way down the wall in a zigzag direction, until it became lost in the sullen waters of the tarn" (pp. 97–98). The fissure, of course, represents the mad line in the self symbolized by the sister's name—Madeline—and also by, as Joseph J. Moldenhauer points out, the family name of "Us-her."[10]

In his article, Moldenhauer cites the pun in the family name as further evidence of the achievement of final unity in the story.[11] However, the narrator's existential context, his way of being-in-the-world, allows for an exactly opposite conclusion in which Roderick Usher operates as a false-self system designed to separate and protect the disembodied narrator from reality. The tarn operates to further reenforce this theme of isolation and separation. The water, of course, creates a mirror image. The fact that the tarn is "black and lurid" and that it exacerbates the narrator's terror indicates the pernicious nature of the truth it holds. Poe's use of this mirror image helps demonstrate his relationship to other major writers of the nineteenth century who were developing the modern existential approach to the human condition. Like Poe in this scene, Kierkegaard uses a mirror image to symbolize the existential situation of the self. "Unhappy mirror," Kierkegaard writes, "that can indeed seize her image but not herself! Unhappy mirror, which cannot hide her image in its secret depths, hide it from the whole world, but on the contrary must betray it to others, as now to me. What agony, if men were made like that! And are there not many people who are like that, who own nothing except in the moment when they show it to others, who grasp only the surface, not the essence, who lose everything if this appears, just as this mirror would lose her image, were she by a single breath to betray her heart to it?"[12] For Kierkegaard, then, the mirror contains the false self subject to immediate dissolution. The real or transcendent self remains outside the mirror's grasp. Referring to earlier work by Freud on the subject,

Laing reaches a similar conclusion. The mirror reveals a false self to the schizoid. But at the same time the appearance of the false self proves the existence of its creator, the "true" self. The schizoid "becomes another person to himself who could look at him from the mirror," writes Laing (*TDS*, p. 117). He notes that if the person could not see himself in the mirror "he himself would be 'gone'; thus he was employing a schizoid presupposition by the help of the mirror, whereby there were two 'hims', one *there* and the other *here*" (*TDS*, p. 117).

In "Usher" the tarn also sustains the narrator's "schizoid presupposition"; it reflects the false self of the House of Usher and its setting. Significantly, after gazing into the tarn the narrator fails to report seeing himself. The tarn, which is connected to the mad line of the house and into which the house will crumble, terrifies the narrator because it assures him that his way of preserving his own existence actually rests upon nothing and that the empty state of his self will continue. Thus, his experience of the tarn includes the sensation of being over a "precipitous brink," a situation redolent of such other Poe stories as "The Imp of the Perverse" and "The Pit and the Pendulum," in which the brink forewarns of a fall into nothingness.[13] "I reined my horse," says the narrator in "Usher," "to the precipitous brink of a black and lurid tarn that lay in unruffled lustre by the dwelling, and gazed down—but with a shudder even more thrilling than before—upon the remodelled and inverted images of the gray sedge, and the ghastly tree-stems, and the vacant and eye-like windows" (p. 96).

A false self also appears in a mirror, although an imaginary one, at the end of "William Wilson." Wilson sees "mine own image" in a mirror that suddenly appears in a room "where none had been perceptible before" (p. 130). Wilson's doppelgänger, or double, operates as the disembodied self, a view supported by the failure of others in the story to perceive its existence as a second Wilson.[14] So, if we understand Wilson existentially as a relationship between a disembodied self and a false-self system, we can also read the story as a study of schizophrenic psychosis. According to Laing, schizophrenia reaches the psychotic stage when the false self achieves enough power to threaten the existence of the true or transcendent self. The false-self system in this condition becomes "extensive" and "autonomous." Its behavior grows increasingly fragmented and incoherent and "all that belongs to it becomes more and more dead, unreal, false, mechanical" (*TDS*, p. 144). Laing's picture of the false-self system in this condition fairly accurately describes Wilson from his youth to the time of the duel with his doppelgänger at the end of the story. Wilson's murder of his double or disembodied self further indicates psychosis. Discussing death in existential rather than physical terms, Laing says that "manifest psychosis" will likely result in an individual who carries through "an attempt to murder his self" (*TDS*, p. 147). The final words of "William Wilson" spoken by the double and italicized by Poe seem to confirm such a reading: "*You have conquered, and I yield. Yet, henceforward art thou also dead—dead to the World, to Heaven, and to Hope! In me didst thou exist—and, in my death, see by this image, which is thine own, how utterly thou hast murdered thyself*" (p. 130). Physically, then, Wilson will survive—but he will survive as a hollow shell without any central core of existence. He will have a mirror existence. As such he will be like the people in Poe's "Man of the Crowd" who lack any existence by themselves. Like the old man in the story who wears a death mask and like the clerks who walk the streets, he will go through life dead to the world.

Taken to its extreme, the process of killing the self becomes perverseness, the force in Poe which, according to Baudelaire, "makes man constantly and simultaneously a murderer and a suicide, an assassin and a hangman."[15] Poe's discussion of "the spirit of PERVERSENESS," which he defines in "The Black Cat" as the "unfathomable longing of the soul *to vex itself*—to offer violence to its own nature," further demonstrates his insight into the sadomasochistic potential of the self (p. 201). Beyond that, however, the battle between the narrator of "The Imp of the Perverse" and his fiend also constitutes one of Poe's greatest insights into the schizophrenic process by illustrating the manner in which transcendence provides the means for what Laing calls "the basic defence, so far as I have been able to see, in every form of psychosis" (*TDS*, pp. 149–150). According to Laing, this "ultimate and most paradoxically absurd defence, beyond which magic defences can go no further," represents the desire of the self to die in order to preserve its existence (*TDS*, p. 149). He writes: "It can be stated in its most general form as: *the denial of being, as a means of preserving being.* The schizophrenic feels he has killed his 'self', and this appears to be in order to avoid being killed. He is dead, in order to remain alive" (*TDS*, p. 150). As Laing fairly states, the theologian Paul Tillich makes a similar case in *The Courage to*

Be. Tillich argues that courage allows the individual to integrate the anxiety of nonbeing into the self in order to achieve a fuller sense of being. The failure of such courage ironically causes the individual to fall into the very thing she or he fears: nonbeing. *"Neurosis,"* Tillich writes, *"is the way of avoiding nonbeing by avoiding being."* [16] He goes on to say, "Pathological anxiety about fate and death impels toward a security which is comparable to the security of a prison. He who lives in this prison is unable to leave the security given to him by his self-imposed limitation. But these limitations are not based on a full awareness of reality. Therefore the security of the neurotic is unrealistic. . . . *Misplaced* fear is a consequence of the pathological form of the anxiety of fate and death." [17]

This sort of prison mentality provides an important insight into the narrator of "The Imp of the Perverse." A criminal and a murderer, the narrator claims to feel safe in the world, which in fact he turns into ever tightening prisons of the self. After committing his crime, his only danger, he says, comes from an imp that can gain control over his body and actions. In existential terms, then, an inner self feels safe from reality but endangered by a false-self system. The inner self craves the security the narrator claims. "I would perpetually catch myself pondering upon my security," he says, "and repeating in a low under-tone, the phrase, 'I am safe.'" But the imp hounds him and he says again, "I am safe—I am safe—yes—if I be not fool enough to make open confession!" (p. 230). An imaginary but uncompromising enemy, the imp reveals a perverseness which, according to the narrator, includes "a strongly antagonistical sentiment" completely opposed to the narrator's well-being (p. 227). The imp eventually achieves control over the narrator's entire perspective on reality, sabotaging any attempt by the narrator to relate to reality through "thought" or "reflection" and diminishing the significance of all other sources of danger. For the narrator the imp then becomes the paramount threat from which to escape, and this can be done only by confessing. The confession neutralizes the power of the imp, disarming it of the weapon it held over the narrator. In effect, the narrator dies to keep from dying. Moreover, the physical extinction seems to fail to arouse a response that would be commensurate with the situation. His attitude toward real death approaches insouciance and indicates the continuing success of his defensive strategy of estranging the self from his body. "To-day," he says, "I wear these chains, and am here! Tomorrow I shall be fetterless! but where?" (p. 230). His question concerning the future implies uncertainty but also contains an element of the expectation of continued survival for the transcendent self despite the imminent doom of the chained body. Even in an actual prison, which represents the culmination of the narrator's basic defensive strategy, he continues to seek deeper inner prisons of the self in which to hide.

Poe's understanding of guilt as a means for the continuation of the inward spiraling of the self toward false security comprises an additional major achievement in this and other stories. In "The Imp of the Perverse," in "The Tell-Tale Heart," and to a certain extent in "The Black Cat," Poe's protagonists confess out of a sense of guilt totally divorced from any genuinely felt grief or sorrow, emotions which suggest an ability to relate to others. Rather, they confess out of a sense of guilt which in itself operates as a further symptom of the disease which initially caused them to murder. Guilt becomes, in Laing's phrase, a "psychic tourniquet" assuring the continued separation of the self from the body (*TDS*, p. 133). "The individual," writes Laing, "feels guilty at daring to be, and doubly guilty at not being, at being too terrified to be, and attempting to murder himself if not biologically, then existentially. His guilt is the urgent factor in preventing active participation in life, and in maintaining the 'self' in isolation, in pushing it into further withdrawal" (*TDS*, p. 157).

Guilt over being and double guilt over wishing not to be partly explain the situation of the narrator in "The Fall of the House of Usher." Functioning as a true self involved in tearing itself apart, the narrator feels guilt as an important motivation in his relationship with Usher. In fact, guilt over neglecting Usher, who "had been one of my boon companions in boyhood" and who still considered the narrator "indeed his only personal friend," helps move him to make the journey (p. 96). Moreover, the House of Usher also functions like a prison where the narrator develops what Laing calls "a pseudo-interpersonal" relationship in which "the self treats the false selves as though they were other people" (*TDS*, p. 74). At first, the narrator seems to find a new security with Usher. He shares music, reading, and even some intimate moments with him. At the same time, however, the futility of such efforts serves to emphasize the extremity of Usher's sickness and to rigidify the estrangement of the two men. "And thus," says the narrator, "as a closer and still closer intimacy admitted me more unreservedly into the recesses of his spirit, the more bitterly did I perceive the futility of all attempt at cheering a mind from which darkness, as if an inherent positive quality, poured forth upon all objects of the moral and physical universe in one unceasing radiation of gloom" (p. 101). In spite of his expression of benevolent intentions, the narrator's attitude toward Usher really demonstrates fear and uncertainty. Clearly, he sees Usher's erratic behavior and sickness as a personal danger to himself. Since existentially the sickness belongs to him, such fears are misplaced but well founded. Furthermore, the steady worsening of Usher's malady in the presence of the narrator suggests that he contributes to Usher's fear and insecurity. A conflict between warring parts of the same mind ineluctably leads to an attempt to achieve security through the death of the self.

Accordingly, Madeline grows increasingly important as the story moves toward its conclusion. She becomes the ultimate symbol of the existential dilemma at the heart of the story—the attempt of the self to preserve its being through its own death. On the level of the story's action she evokes horror because of her bloody return from the tomb. But the lasting terror that sustains the melodrama of her physical return comes from the subsurface psychological drama of the story. On this level, we see that the death-in-life relationship of Usher and the narrator serves as the more horrible but truer tomb from which she rises. She comes to represent the extension of a schizoid relationship between a disembodied and a false self. The temporal coincidence of her debilitation soon after the narrator's arrival indicates her intimate involvement in the Usher-narrator relationship as it draws closer to a final resolution. As a symbol of death-in-life and of the murder of the self, she appropriately takes the form of a ghost. Her initial appearance in the story occurs in a scene that reads almost like a burlesque of a ghost story. "While he spoke," writes Poe, "the lady Madeline (for so she was called) passed slowly through a remote portion of the apartment, and, without having noticed my presence, disappeared. I regarded her with an utter astonishment not unmingled with dread—and yet I found it impossible to account for such feelings" (p. 101). As a ghost she is literally "sick unto death," as in "The Pit and the Pendulum," suffering from a disease the cause of which "had long baffled the skill of her physicians" because, we can assume, it would be indiscernible to ordinary doctors (p. 101).

At the same time, however, Usher's own song, "The Haunted Palace," and the other elements of the story suggest that Madeline's ghostliness also serves to impugn Usher's and the narrator's full humanity. Symbolizing the psychological truth of the way in which the narrator and Usher exist for each other, Madeline helps reveal that both are figments of the same imagination. In Laing's term they are phantoms, like the imp of the perverse. A creation of the self, the phantom terrorizes the self. It allows the transcendent self to shun any contact with the world that is real to others while further contributing to the situation of confusion and uncertainty of the false self. Laing writes: "Moreover, the self-self relationship provides the internal setting for violent attacks upon warring phantoms inside, experienced as having a sort of phantom concreteness. It is in fact such attacks from such inner phantoms that compel the individual to say he has been murdered, or that 'he' has murdered his 'self'" (*TDS*, p. 158). Similarly, in the Ethelred story that the narrator reads to Usher, a dragon—another imaginary enemy symbolizing a psychic inability to confront real danger—significantly shares the same house or mind with a hermit or sealed-up inner self and must be slain, finally, by the artificial figure of a knight. The conclusion of "Usher," including Madeline's entombment, return, and final demise with Usher, marks the realization on the level of action of the existential conflict between life and death that runs throughout the story. The frantic escape of the narrator may be the most terrifying action of all because it implies that the process of internal disintegration will continue beyond the time of the story.

In a sense, the "*way of avoiding nonbeing by avoiding being*," to repeat Tillich's phrase, becomes in Poe the "sickness unto death," although most readers probably associate the biblical phrase with the use Kierkegaard makes of it. For Kierkegaard, the sickness unto death is the despair of sufferers who are denied the death for which they yearn. "It is in this last sense," he writes, "that despair is the sickness unto death, this agonizing contradiction, this sickness in the self, everlastingly to die, to die and yet not to die, to die the death. For dying means that it is all over, but dying the death means to live to experience death; and if for a single instant this experience is possible, it is tantamount to experiencing it forever."[18] Poe discusses the sickness unto death in a similar fashion in "The Pit and the Pendulum," in which the narrator begins his story with these very words: "I was sick—sick unto death with that long agony" (p. 180).[19] For Kierkegaard and to some extent for Poe, the "sickness" describes the dread of the individual who realizes the internal existence of what Tillich calls "the eternal now," the moment in which the temporal and the eternal coincide. But, of course, the sickness therefore also describes the existential basis of schizophrenia as Laing explains it. In this context, the sickness becomes the condition of a transcendent or disembodied self that has died the death, that has experienced death but survives. Laing writes that, for the self withdrawing from reality to protect itself, "the place of safety of the self becomes a prison. Its would-be haven becomes a hell." "It ceases," he continues, "even to have the safety of a solitary cell. Its own enclave becomes a torture chamber. The inner self is persecuted within this chamber by split concretized parts of itself or by its own phantoms which have become uncontrollable" (*TDS*, p. 162).

In *The Politics of Experience* Laing makes the Kierkegaardian argument that the kind of experience of dread just described tends to prove our potential for salvation. Schizophrenia, he says, becomes the means for a "transcendental experience," a "journey of initiation." The transcendent self, he argues, provides a vehicle for escape from an insane society that forces its citizens to accept mendacious standards of normality and that condones forms of insanity judged socially necessary. "Madness," he writes, "need not be all breakdown. It may also be breakthrough. It is potentially liberation and renewal as well as enslavement and existential death."[20] Poe to some extent, of course, shares Laing's view of madness as breakthrough. But he seems far less certain about the nature of the reality beyond that breakthrough. Like Laing, Poe may feel that schizophrenia becomes in the modern age *a special strategy that a person invents to live in an unlivable situation*—that a modern individual suffers from a "socially conditioned illusion" that he exists as a person, whereas in fact he is "at least a double absence, haunted by the ghost of his own murdered self" and the ghost of others.[21] Poe also might have agreed with Laing when Laing says that we all have become mad in one way or another. But, unlike Laing, Poe seems uncertain that there is anything else. He seems to feel that if, like the narrator of "Usher," we break through our prisons, on the outside we will find only another prison. Certainly in "The Pit and the Pendulum," as G. R. Thompson argues, Poe proffers little over which to feel optimistic. In the tales but also in *Eureka*, as Thompson says, Poe's "design of the Universe is but a symmetrical cycle of journeys out of, and back into, Void."[22]

Perhaps the modern liberal imagination begins where Poe

and Laing end—with the awareness of the void but also with the sense of an obligation to live with it as one must live with one's freedom. The need to deal with the void while accepting responsibility for one's involvement in reality and experience constitutes what Trilling calls moral realism and tragedy. Speaking from the vantage point of an age in which the void has become almost a cliché, I find the quality of moral realism and tragedy sorely lacking in Poe. Similarly, Laing seems to such liberal critics as Trilling overly simple in his basic disregard of "the reality principle" and of "the complex psychic dynamics which Freud explicated."[23]

The questions Trilling and others ask of Laing, the Transcendentalists of the mid nineteenth century asked of themselves. The attempt to achieve an authentic identity without turning inward toward perversity, as did Poe, while still avoiding the loss of one's self in the crowd and maintaining one's relationship to both culture and society was a perennial and central paradox for the Transcendentalists. In a sense, it involved their attempt to reconcile a liberal individualism, which was of course alien to Poe's consciousness, with an elevation of the self, a venture which led Poe to seek in the self a means for realizing some form of ultimate escape. As already noted, this indicates not only an artistic and cultural decision but a political action as well. It was a form of rebellion that seemed to cast Poe out of the major stream of our intellectual and cultural tradition—that is until our own time, when the radical nature of his decision and the extremity of his action make him especially relevant to some recent modes of rebellion.

℘ Chapter 3
Emerson and Brownson:
The scholar, the self, and society

"The Puritan's dilemma," according to Sacvan Bercovitch, "was that the way from the self necessarily led through the self; occasionally, the struggle became so severe that he could resolve it only by abandoning all hope, or else . . . by leaping, self and all, directly to Christ. For the Romantic, the way to the self led through the precursor poet. Only the strongest did not abandon either poetry or the self."[1] In some ways this crisis of the self reached an even greater critical intensity for the descendants of the Puritans, the Transcendentalists. The Transcendentalists had to work through the same paradox of the self and the same dilemmas involving the self and society. However, they had the added burden of confronting these issues in the context of a secular culture which presented many of them with the problem of translating the word "soul" into "self" in a meaningful way. As Lawrence Buell notes, for some critics of the age the "soul" had become "self."[2] The Transcendentalists' crisis of self and of identity of course continues to our own day, a fact which partly accounts for the kind of questions some of our literary and cultural critics tend to ask of the period.

Moreover, this issue of the self relates to other questions and issues of tangible relevance to our own day. "By now," writes Perry Miller, "almost as much has been written about the New England Transcendentalists as they ever wrote by themselves. They attract attention not only because they do not occupy a place in our intellectual history but even more because they speak for an important mood in the spiritual life of the Republic—a mood that has subsequently become, periodically, vocal."[3] This mood of course defies simple definition, but we know that it has repeated itself throughout our history as what Miller calls "the rift between generations."[4] We have gone through other periods of generational conflict marked by the rebellion of youth acting with the greatest passion in the name of heady idealism and benevolent reform. Of course, in the light of what we have said about Poe, we need to emphasize that this form of the youth culture is characterized most strongly by its identification with the cultural mainstream. These youth never really stopped belonging, so to speak, to the family of the dominant culture. Poe, on the other hand, embodied an artistic and alien consciousness that represents a form of psychological and cultural rebellion that differs markedly from the reformist orientation of the Transcendentalists. As Buell says, "In its liberal, upper-middle-class origins and in its short-lived but colorful exuberance, marked by insistence upon personal freedom and spiritual reform, the Transcendentalist movement strongly resembles the revolution of sensibility which we have been witnessing among educated young people in our own time."[5]

Thus, the Transcendentalists present us with an early insight into and version of the dynamics of what appears to be an interesting form of rebelliousness done in the name of an inspirational inheritance of ambitious parental idealism. In a sense, one generation sees itself in terms of the ideal self—an American self—articulated by an earlier generation. In this regard the Transcendental experience further prefigures intellectual and moral events of our recent period of the 1950s and 1960s, in which the reformist impulse of one generation evolved into and inspired a wave of passionate radical zeal among the young, who wished to put into action the ideals and moral concepts they had been taught.[6]

Henry Nash Smith, in his essay "The American Scholar Today," also sees important parallels between Emerson's era and our own. Moreover, in Smith's perspective and attitude one finds a further example of the phenomenon of a liberal consciousness whose sympathy for socially critical and reform-oriented projects in a sense set the stage for later youthful idealism and activism. Thus, Smith expresses special concern about the tendency in his own culture toward conformity, and he notes a similarity in this regard between Emerson's culture and our own. He notes and seems to support studies by established and respectable scholars and writers who also perceive such conformist trends in contemporary culture and seem alarmed by them.[7] There are books, he says, like *White Collar* by C. Wright Mills and *The Organization Man* by William H. Whyte, Jr., which are based on "empirical data drawn from formal survey and statistical tables," as well as a second category of books that "are more personal and hortatory."

"But," he writes, "they all say in effect that the rudimentary commercial interests which Emerson identified with State Street and Quincy capitalists have developed in the twentieth century into the imposing and apparently monolithic structures of modern American business."[8]

Significantly, while strongly sympathetic to the situation of the young in such an era and highly supportive of attempts to counter such dehumanizing cultural trends, Smith in his essay of 1963 finds it impossible to avoid mentioning his ineluctable separation from the younger generation of rebels. He says, "I have the impulse to add one further comment for the benefit of those who share with me the status of pillars of the Establishment. Whereas the young men with knives in their brains are suffering the agonies of choice, we are committed, long ago, by time and habit if by nothing else. Whether we like it or not, we have a stake in society as a going concern; we are the people who keep it going."[9] He goes on to add a sort of apology as one of the "elders" who helped make the current situation. It is necessary for one's "comfort," he says, to "believe in the world and the society we have created and are therefore responsible for."[10]

Smith's experience and analysis further the comparison of the emergence of Transcendentalism from Unitarianism with the rise, more recently, of a form of radicalism from the doctrines and values of contemporary liberalism. The similarity suggests that the radical movements and so-called cultural revolution of the sixties can be seen as an extension of what Lionel Trilling calls "the liberal imagination" as that imagination is delineated not only in Trilling's work but in the values and ideals of such other writers as Smith and David Riesman. Like these other writers we find in Trilling much that sympathizes with rebellion. Accordingly, much of his own social, literary, and cultural criticism anticipates some of the concerns of the sixties. This includes the fear that he repeatedly expresses of the diminution of individual freedom and selfhood. It also includes a kind of spiritual concern that helped form the sixties mood. When Trilling, for example, discusses Henry James as a moral imagination that sees differences but still manages to love, he in fact captures some of the moral flavor so much a part of the 1960s fervor.[11] As with so many other liberals, such as Riesman and Smith, Trilling's own revolt against the monotony, conformity, and sterility of his age gave direction and force to the impulse for change which broke into more extreme rebellion in the sixties. Values elevating autonomy, individuality, moral realism, artistic imagination, and creativity and love can easily be read as exhortations to achieve and follow a sense of one's self and one's identity.[12]

In addition, in his analysis of Herbert Marcuse, a major force in the radical thought of the 1960s, Trilling undermines a vital aspect of Marcuse's position by demonstrating its similarity to traditional liberal thought about culture and individual character formation. He emphasizes that beneath Marcuse's radical rhetoric resides a concern "with the devolution of the power of the superego, which he sees as resulting in a deplorably lowered degree of individuality and autonomy."[13] Thus, in Trilling's interpretation, Marcuse shares with tamer liberals a passion for traditional character-structured individualism. Trilling perceives this issue of individual character formation as one of the key themes marking the division between generations. It relates in a vital way to other key issues concerning work and leisure, cultural priorities, individual achievement versus equality.

However, the debate was not confined simply to different sides of the generation gap. As already noted, it was basically a generational conflict over issues, ideas, and style. At the same time, however, it makes sense that the conflict would express itself within the ranks of the uninitiated as a sort of extension among the young within the family of the dispute. And so it did. As with the Transcendentalists in an earlier century, the recent radicals and reformers divided among themselves over what was perhaps the most basic issue of all, involving the meaning of both transcendence and freedom as those concepts relate to the effort to reform society and the character of the people within it. Moreover, with their middle-class origins and liberal backgrounds, these reformers intellectually, emotionally, and physically tended—for reasons of propinquity and access—to focus many of their issues and themes upon what is probably the most liberal institution in our society, the university. The division over the role of the university within the society and the culture included disagreement over the even more immediate issue of the role of the scholar, using the word "scholar" in the two intimately related ways Emerson tended to use it—literally as the young person in school working to achieve a sense of identity and a place in the culture and symbolically as the unique individual learner striving to unite soul and self, mind and body, in a life of meaningful thought and action. In Emerson's own time, of course, he was central to an important debate among the Transcendentalists over the scholar and education. That earlier debate assumed certain patterns of division among the Transcendentalists that in some ways prefigured the division among today's radical and reform groups.

In the more recent debate we find, on the one hand, reformers oriented toward the elevation of individualism and personal identity as major values in education. They espoused programs of self-direction and individual initiative that naturally tended to be derived from the existential and psychological works of such thinkers as Laing and Carl Rogers. On the other hand, social, political, and group consciousness tended to dominate the second faction. They argued for the reorientation of academic values and standards toward sexual and racial equality, the community, justice, and other issues related to social and political conscience. One placed the individual at the center of the universe while the other stressed social and communal hegemony. One emphasized personal freedom, the other social equality and ties. Clearly, both groups frequently converged over such specific issues as minority and feminist rights, the democratization of the decision-making process, the mitigation of rigid academic forms and structures, and the development of alternative approaches to education. But beneath such unanimity were basic differences over emphasis, values, and philosophy that perpetuated conflict and tension. Moreover, the same pattern of unity and disagreement involving these basic dichotomies could be found in reform movements in other institutions throughout the social structure. Among the young, however, who were so involved in shaping their own identities as scholars and people, the desire to change and even revolutionize the university was most intensely felt. It was not just that the university, like the family, was an institution that most immediately affected them and upon which they could exert a strong influence. It was also that these institutions in general seemed to be the most tolerant of the radical and reformist impulse. In any case, further study of the theoretical and philosophical debate over the purpose and function of education and the role of the scholar as it first manifested itself in its modern form in the Emerson-Brownson debate should prove useful in helping us understand the issues in their current stage.

For the ten years prior to his conversion to Catholicism in 1844, Orestes Brownson was a leader in the Transcendentalist wars against the Lockean foundations of Unitarianism, external authority, intellectual elitism, and economic, social, and political inequality. As a forceful and outspoken Transcendentalist, Brownson found much in Emerson's position on the scholar with which to agree, especially when it came to defending Emerson against attack from outside the movement. Writing in his own *Boston Quarterly Review* in October 1838, Brownson strongly defended the purpose behind Emerson's essay on "The American Scholar." He described the essay as a major attempt to inveigle scholars into freeing their souls so their minds could follow. "The great object he is laboring to accomplish," Brownson writes, "is one in which he should receive the hearty cooperation of every American scholar, of every friend of truth, freedom, piety and virtue." Brownson goes on to say that Emerson's real object was "to induce men to think for themselves on all subjects, and to speak from their own full hearts and earnest convictions. His object is to make men scorn to be slaves to routine, to custom, to established creeds, to public opinion, to the great names of this age, of this country, or of any other" (p. 199).

Moreover, Brownson perceived with approval the pragmatic strain in Emerson's thought. He writes of Emerson: "He cannot bear the idea that a man comes into the world today with the field of truth monopolized and foreclosed. To every man lies open the whole field of truth, in morals, in politics, in science, in theology, in philosophy. The labors of past ages, the revelations of prophets and bards, the discoveries of the scientific and philosophic, are not to be regarded as superseding our own exertions and inquiries, as impediments to the free action of our own minds, but merely as helps, as provocations to the freest and fullest spiritual action of which God has made us capable." (p. 199).

However, even during this period of deep allegiance to Transcendentalism, Brownson recognized, as Perry Miller states, an "incipient disagreement" with Emerson over basic questions (p. 431). Also, as A. Robert Caponigri argues in a brilliant essay, Emerson and Brownson had basic differences from the beginning over issues that emerged originally out of the Protestant Reformation concerning humanity's relationship to history and to God.[14] But equally profound differences existed on an emotional and visceral level.

Born and raised in poverty in rural Vermont, Brownson instinctively identified with "the people," the masses with whom Emerson could rarely be comfortable. In a review of Emerson's Dartmouth address on "Literary Ethics," Brownson castigated

Emerson for putting the scholar before the country. "The scholar," he writes, "must have an end to which his scholarship serves as a means" (p. 432). For Brownson the end for which scholarship served as the means involved subverting the importance of scholarship to the greater needs of the people. In order to perceive and understand these needs, the scholar must become one of the people. "We can make the people listen to us," he writes, "only so far as we are one of them" (p. 432). He therefore rejected what he perceived as Emerson's "notion that the scholar must be a solitary soul, living apart and in himself alone; that he must shun the multitude and mingle never in the crowd, or if he mingle, never as one of the crowd" (p. 432). Brownson's reading of Emerson's ideas here compares to criticism of Emerson made by W. H. Channing in a review of "The American Scholar," in which he writes, "Not as a scholar, not with a view to literary labor, not as an artist, must he go out among men—but as a brother man." [15]

Clearly overlooking much in Emerson's thought that called for action and synthesis, Brownson also said Emerson tended "to concentrate the scholar entirely within himself, to make him a mere individual, without connexions or sympathies with his race; and to make him utter his own individualized life, not the life of the nation, much less the universal life of Humanity" (p. 432). As part of the people, the scholar would learn from the people and then would be able to express their natural genius. The scholar, then, would function as a midwife to democratic consciousness. "American scholars we shall have," Brownson writes, "but only in proportion as the scholar weds himself to American principles and becomes the interpreter of American life" (p. 433).

Brownson's interpretation of "Literary Ethics" probably says more about his own views than it does about Emerson or the essay.[16] The review reflects Brownson's own attitudes about the role of the scholar and the university—attitudes that differed markedly from Emerson's more complex position. Thus, in sharp contrast to Emerson, who disliked writing to President Van Buren on behalf of the displaced Cherokees of Georgia and who hated "goodies" and "the goodness that preaches," Brownson believed that scholars and the very institutions of learning needed to sacrifice their own interests and values to help the deprived and the underprivileged. He argued that scholars could save themselves only by trying to save the less fortunate. Like many modern radicals and reformers, he saw education as a tool for social, political, and economic progress in the form of advancing equality. Scholars, he felt, must first look toward the slums in the cities and the thickening malaise of the "laboring classes" before looking within themselves for ultimate truth.

Accordingly, Brownson's arguments for institutional reform vaticinated modern modes of radical conscience. In the same issue of the journal in which he expressed some of his uncertainty over the ultimate veracity of Emerson's opinions on the scholar, Brownson also struck almost virulently at Andrews Norton, the avatar of all that was held most sacred by the Unitarians, including the Harvard tradition. For Brownson, Norton and his views embodied that university and its faults. Brownson maintained that Harvard failed to recognize its obligations to the poor and to the community. The institution placed its own values, standards, and well-being above the best interests of all the people. Instead of working to serve the masses, it endeavored to either disregard or repress them. For Brownson, an elitist institution with special privileges over the people represented a perversion of the natural, moral, and humanitarian order of things. "The history," he writes, "of the University, in which our author is or was a professor, together with that of her favorite sons, may tend to confirm this conclusion, to which invincible logic conducts us. That University, we believe, has not of late years been renowned for her reverence for the people, her faith in democratic institutions, or her efforts to establish universal suffrage and equal rights. We have not heard that she takes any particular pains to educate her sons in harmony with those free principles which are the just pride of all true Americans" (p. 209).

The vituperation of Brownson's attack on Harvard as an undemocratic and socially irresponsible institution and on Norton as its symbol dramatizes his divergence in style, philosophy, and purpose from Emerson as well. Perry Miller succinctly summarizes Brownson's purposes. Miller says, "So that there might be no mistake about what he intended *The Boston Quarterly Review* to do," Brownson chose to respond to a published attack on Emerson's *Nature* by Francis Bowen, a Harvard professor and a spokesman for the respectable and conservative reaction to Transcendentalism. Noting that Brownson "thus stepped into the arena where Emerson would not deign to enter," Miller writes, "But Brownson's line of attack was not exactly what Emerson would have taken had he condescended to fight: the difference between Unitarian sensationalism and Transcendental institutionalism was here presented, not as a contrast between the bookworm and Man Think-ing, but as the clash of aristocracy and democracy" (p. 183). Ac-cordingly, Brownson writes in his review, "Philosophy is not needed by the masses but they who separate themselves from the masses, and who believe that the masses are entirely depen-dent on them for truth and virtue, need it, to bring them back, and bind them again to the universal Humanity" (p. 185). Ob-viously, Brownson's devotion to the masses at the time of his article on Bowen constitutes a major divergence of view from Emerson.[17] Still, Brownson's rhetorical strategy in this essay in which he turned the tables on the conservatives represents an impressive feat. His assertion of the true Americanism of the mass-es involved the imputation of an un-American quality to the re-spectable elite. As Miller writes, "The charge was indeed pressed home: it was now the respectable and rational disciples of Locke who found themselves indicted as un-American and their vaunted 'common sense' was exposed as a dodge for denying the rights of the masses" (p. 183).

In effect Brownson virtually proffered a new hierarchy in which common sense as the proclaimed domain of the masses achieves a special place because it has access to what he vaguely describes as higher forms of "truths." These truths are accessible to the commonsensical form of "spontaneous reason," which "de-velops itself in all men" and "furnishes the universal beliefs of mankind," in contrast to the philosophically oriented "reflective reason," which awakens in only a few people in any society (p. 185). If common sense is the universal form of reason, the people can serve as a better source of authority for truths than philoso-phers who can be corrupted by aristocratic notions and institu-tions. "Nor let it be supposed that we would debar the people at large from the truths the philosopher professes to have demon-strated," writes Brownson. "These truths are not the peculiar pos-session of the philosopher. They are the truths of the universal reason, and are the property alike of all men. They are taught to all men by the spontaneous reason, which is the same in kind in every man. These truths are not the philosophy. Philosophy is the explanation and verification of them. The masses, who see nothing mysterious in these truths, and who have never thought of questioning them, do not wish to have them explained or veri-fied. The explanation and verification, which is philosophy, are unintelligible to them. But the truths themselves, are not unintel-ligible to them" (pp. 183–184).

The moral passion and anger over poverty that stimulate Brownson's writing sometimes get diffused in his tendency to deal with the abstractions that concern his intellectual audience. He is most impressive when he writes directly about the conditions of the poor, especially the young and their inadequate education under poverty. "The masses," he writes, "after the flesh, it must be admitted, are surrounded with unwholesome influences, and provided with most wretched teachers. They must then be filled with evil thoughts and false notions. Their beliefs, their hopes and fears, likes, and dislikes, are deserving no respect. Hence, on the one hand, the contempt of the masses manifested by so large a portion of the educated, even in democratic America, and, on the other hand, the pity and commiseration, the great condescension, and vast amount of baby-talk, which equally characterize another, but more kind-hearted, portion of the more favored classes" (p. 184). Such passages indicate how, in this phase of his thinking, Brownson came to rely heavily upon collective and organized modes of reform in contrast to the kind of "self-reliance" Emerson so strongly espoused. As Americo D. Lapati says, "Brownson found it necessary to abandon his approach to social reform by individual moral reform; for he saw that social conditions could influence moral behavior. It was useless to preach the power of prayer when the power to earn a living did not exist. Economic conditions brought on by the Panic of 1837— the failure and suspension of banks, the closing of factories, and depression putting many laborers out of work—convinced him that action was necessary. Identifying the Whigs as the party of the greedy plutocracy, he backed the Democratic Party as the laboring man's hope for social and economic progress."[18]

However, contained within such passion for collective action was an incipient form of determinism—a belief in the masses that proclaims their superiority in terms of their inevitable victory, a victory that will justify the faith placed in them. Accordingly, in his discussion of Bowen, Brownson moves from a kind of moral and mental elevation of the masses to a sense of their destiny and power. "The world," he writes, "is filled with commotions. The masses are heaving and rolling, like a mighty river, swollen with recent rains, and snows dissolving on the mountains, onward to a distant and unknown ocean. There are those among us, who stand awe-struck, who stand amazed. What means this heaving and onward rolling? Whither tend these mighty masses of human beings? Will they sweep away every fixture, every house and barn, every mark of civilization? Where will they end? In what will they end? Shall we rush before them and attempt to stay their progress? Or shall we fall into their ranks and on with them to their goal?" (pp. 185–186). There is a sense of naturalism in this redolent of what Dreiser would write decades later in "The Myth of Individuality" and on the condition of the self in the hostile urban environment.

Such determinism would seem to contradict the earlier faith Brownson had placed in mass education to enable each individual to achieve some degree of independence and control over the future. Sounding in 1865 much like Dreiser, Brownson writes in *The American Republic*, "Men are little moved by mere reasoning, however clear and convincing it may be. They are moved by their affections, passions, instincts, and habits. Routine is more powerful with them than logic. A few are greedy of novelties and are always for trying experiments; but the great body of the people of all nations have an invincible repugnance to abandon what they know for what they know not. They are, to a great extent, the slaves of their own apathy and will not make the necessary exertion to change their existing mode of life, even for a better one. Interest itself is powerless before their indolence, prejudice, habits, and usages."[19] While indicating the development of this form of determinism in Brownson, we should not forget that, famous for his changes of opinion and position, he also went through a period of espousing a doctrine of Christian liberty that at times made him seem almost more individualistic than Emerson.[20]

Like Brownson in the last century, many contemporary critics dismiss the importance to Emerson of the relationship between the self and society. As noted earlier, Quentin Anderson in particular sees Emerson's concern for the temple of the self as a withdrawal inward from social and political reality. Emerson's mode of "self-validation," he feels, took the form of an "imperial self" enabling him to "announce man's participation in divinity as not merely analogous but real. Individuals were His only voice on earth. The only authority was within. We all became actors and speculators in our private theater."[21] However, where Anderson sees an Emersonian imperial self that involves a "coming out of culture," James M. Cox sees exactly the opposite, "a making culture possible."[22] Such an interpretation of Emerson as ineluctably tied to the idea and concept of America does not mean that he had the kind of social consciousness one finds in Brownson. Emerson's choices were not limited to, on the one hand, an inward turn of the imperial self resulting in, as Frederick Hoffman says, blindly dogmatic assertions of the self or, on the other hand, a narrow one-dimensional view of culture as simply a manifestation of economic and social forces.[23] Instead of limiting himself to these two choices Emerson chose another way of thinking and of perceiving that involved a highly creative and symbolic relationship between the self and American culture. As Bercovitch says, for Emerson "arrogating the meaning of America" and assuming responsibility as "the keeper of the dream" involved a process of establishing an identity in terms of the culture itself.[24] The culture in its relationship with the self helped free the imagination.

It is with this sort of understanding of the relationship between self and culture that Emerson pursued his concept of "The American Scholar." The path for the self is intertwined with the direction of the culture. The program for the self also reads as a program and a project for the national culture. Clearly, Emerson anticipates and in a sense even serves as a model for the kind of program for national culture and character adumbrated by Whitman. The speaker for this program, of course, will play a crucial role in history. The paradox involves the need for the individual self to emerge out of the interplay between culture and character, between conditions and self. The true American self would have to emerge out of the right culture to produce it but, at the same time, the ideal American culture also required the forceful leadership of a symbolic self and hero. This situation presented the American scholar with a special challenge and mission. For Emerson the scholar could deal with these unavoidable tensions and difficulties involved in the emergence of the true American prophet. As Bercovitch says, "He expressed his faith most fully in 'The American Scholar.'"[25]

Accordingly, Emerson had to temper his talk on the scholar with the right mixture of rebellious individualism and cultural commitment. Emerson the rebel calls for a "self-relying and self-directed" scholar to exist in a state of "virtual hostility" toward the public and to "defer never to the popular cry."[26] Sounding like Carlyle in his attack on the public and anticipating similar cries in our own day, he writes, "Men are become of no account. Men in history, men in the world of to-day, are bugs, are spawn, and are called 'the mass' and 'the herd'" (p. 106). The masses, he says, have become freaks. He writes, "The state of society is one in which the members have suffered amputation from the trunk, and strut about so many walking monsters,—a good finger, a neck, a stomach, an elbow, but never a man. Man is thus meta-morphosed into a thing, into many things" (p. 83).

This modern picture of the desperate condition of American society provides some measure of Emerson's faith in the scholar. For it indicates not only the enormous challenge and the importance of the scholar's mission but also Emerson's belief in the scholar's power and potential. Because Emerson sees the crisis not in terms of economics and sociology but in terms of the mind and soul, the scholar becomes the individual best trained and suited to lead the revolution necessary for the salvation of society. For this would be a revolution of culture and of the mind. "This revolution," says Emerson, "is to be wrought by the gradual domestication of the idea of Culture. The main enterprise of the world for splendor, for extent, is the upbuilding of a man" (p. 107). For Emerson, the scholar thinking will become an example for others "to speculate or *see*" anew (p. 94). Moreover, Emerson here clearly means vision in an active sense, not as we now think of being spectators of a sport or speculators who fail to earn their own way. He thinks of vision as an instrument of the "soul active" that creates through the way in which it sees. Characteristically, while Brownson attacks Harvard for failing in its duties to help the victims of the urban environment, Emerson attacks the tendency to stifle the creative and life-enhancing impulse in the individual self. Colleges, he insists, "only highly serve us when they aim not to drill, but to create" (p. 93). The whole essay, in a sense, delineates a program for creative thinking that can lead to creative living. "In the right state he is *Man Thinking*," Emerson says of the scholar. "In the degenerate state, when the victim of society, he tends to become a mere thinker, or still worse, the parrot of other men's thinking" (p. 84). The American scholar, then, has the cultural mission to inspire a symbolic, open, mythic mode of thought that cultivates a free consciousness as opposed to a one-dimensional, oppressively prosaic, morally absolutist, and painfully literal mode of thought that ultimately undermines individual freedom in spite of what may be its good intentions.

Thus, Emerson in his position on the American scholar does constitute a challenge to the kind of socially oriented program for education and for the impoverished masses adumbrated by Brownson. In that argument Emerson represents the elevation of the individual self. At the same time, we must remember that this is an individual self whose meaning and definition are derived from its sense of cultural connection and continuity. Nevertheless, in his avowed commitment to individual self-reliance, nonconformity, and heroic achievement, Emerson disagreed with the kind of radical egalitarianism espoused so strongly for a period by Brownson. In his total commitment to achieving the highest individual potential Emerson, according to F. O. Matthiessen, is more representative of the mind and culture of the so-called American Renaissance. Matthiessen writes, "Emerson, Hawthorne, Thoreau, Whitman and Melville all wrote literature for democracy in a double sense. They felt that it was incumbent upon their generation to give fulfillment to the potentialities freed by the Revolution, to provide a culture commensurate with America's political opportunity. Their tones were sometimes optimistic, sometimes blatantly, even dangerously expansive, sometimes disillusioned, even despairing, but what emerges from the total pattern of their achievement—if we will make the effort to repossess it—is literature for our democracy. In reading the lyric, heroic, and tragic expression of our first great age, we can feel the challenge of our still undiminished resources."[27] For Matthiessen a major purpose behind his classic study involves his attempt to revivify for our own age the idea of a literature for our democracy.

Matthiessen succeeds in his self-imposed mission to deal in his own day and work with the ideal established by Emerson in "The American Scholar"—to be both universal and uniquely outstanding and to feel in one's relationship to "the people" the additional responsibility of rising to one's highest potential of achievement. Today, of course, the difficulty of meeting those demands probably seems even greater than in his era. Our democracy seems more disorderly. Our technology continues to reign. Moreover Emerson, with his faith and optimism, now seems quite distant from an atomic age of terror with its recent history of holocaust and genocide. But there also may be more in him for us to consider than we have realized. Emerson's response to history and calamity involved action and the assertion of individual effort to fulfill the promise of life and creation. "It is a mischievous notion," he writes, "that we are come too late into nature; that the world was finished a long time ago. As the world was plastic and fluid in the hands of God, so it is ever to so much of his attributes as we bring to it" (p. 105). Emerson's humanistic and pragmatic demand that each individual must take the responsibility for contributing to an incomplete and open world increases the significance of each individual's involvement in life. As the person endowed with a special gift to see and understand what is going on and to distinguish, in Emerson's phrase, "that a popgun is a popgun, though the ancient and honorable of the earth affirm it to be the crack of doom" (p. 102), the American scholar's responsibility and obligation remain significant. In addition, for the scholar this means in part that the life of the mind cannot be divorced from action. The separation of these realms causes death for the self and for one's culture. Emerson writes, "Action is with the scholar subordinate, but it is essential. Without it he is not yet man. Without it thought can never ripen into truth. Whilst the world hangs before the eye as a cloud of beauty, we cannot even see its beauty. Inaction is cowardice, but there can be no scholar without the heroic mind. The preamble of thought, the transition through which it passes from the unconscious to the conscious, is action. Only so much do I know, as I have lived. Instantly we know whose words are loaded with life, and whose not" (pp. 94–95). Thus, Emerson connects his philosophy of the self and language to his philosophy of a democratic culture. He says that dead words and artificial ideas and beliefs will destroy such a culture, while language that reflects mass thought and mob psychology will destroy the individual. He cannot be faulted, I think, for our own failure to understand and to act upon the prescience of his philosphy.

Chapter 4
Whitman: Culture and self

Many of the themes we have discussed so far—such as the relationship of modern consciousness and American character and values, the growth of conflicting concepts of liberty in the form of pragmatic individualism as opposed to programs for self-realization, the conflict over priorities within radical and reform movements, the inherent tension in our democracy between the individual and the masses and between freedom and culture—come together in the life and work of Walt Whitman. This can be seen even in what others have said and written about him. Thus, in a collection of essays published in honor of the eminent Whitman scholar, Gay Wilson Allen, Edwin Haviland Miller discusses in depth one side of Whitman in "The Radical Vision of Whitman and Pollock." Miller, who edited the collection, opens his essay by saying that "Walt Whitman and Jackson Pollock are undoubtedly our most radical artists."[1] The article that immediately follows, by poet Robert Duncan, however, compares the American bard with Dante. "Whitman, like Dante," says Duncan, "projected a poem central to his civilization."[2] The juxtaposition of such contrasting views dramatizes Whitman's genius for symbolizing and espousing both radical and centralist positions on culture and politics. For Whitman was both "most radical" and "central"; he was the Pollock and the Dante of his age and country. A revolutionary who had deracinated the old and created the new, in *Democratic Vistas* Whitman also, as Duncan says, "like Dante in *De Monarchia* had written a definitive—even *the* definitive—politics of his time."[3] Part of Whitman, then, leaned toward a traditional concept of culture as a set of beliefs, ideals, and symbols that imposed meaning on experience for the American people as Americans. In this sense, Whitman believed in the past and in the obligation to transmit the best of an established liberal democratic tradition to his own and future generations. This part of Whitman saw every American as the benefactor of a special cultural inheritance that constituted a determining force in the shaping of a distinctive

American "personality" and a superior American "race." On the other hand, we also know of another Whitman, who deprecated all tradition as unduly impeding the individual from rising to a new transcendence. This second Whitman, who became the hero of American beats and radicals, saw culture as repressive. For this Whitman, the new American in a new democracy needed to go beyond cultural inhibitions and restraints. Whitman's approach to culture included both these positions in the form of a dialectic that was consistent with the way he dealt with most issues.[4]

The division in Whitman's mind over the relevance and significance of cultural authority and tradition remains a major concern. In fact, for many today the challenge posed to what Eugene Goodheart calls "the custodians of the cultural tradition" by the "radical conscience" may constitute the most important factor shaping contemporary cultural life.[5] For the extreme opponents of authority and tradition, the very concept of dialogue, which traditional liberals believe to be basic to any definition of culture, implies both psychological and social repression. Thus, in Whitman we get the elements for the kind of deadlock we discussed between radicals and liberals and between generations during both the Transcendentalist era and our own.

In the following pages I hope to show the ways in which Whitman's works, when taken from the perspective of the contemporary humanist, anticipate modern radicals and avant-gardists who, according to intellectual historian Hayden White, "attempt to take reality by storm, to seize it immediate and pure and liberate it from the constraints of merely fictive truths and generalizations"—thereby forming a major "attack upon civilization" as we know it.[6] At the same time, I shall try to indicate how such views existed for Whitman in a dynamic dialectical relationship with a complex set of political, religious, and philosophical ideas that constitute an important countercommitment to a cultural tradition which had intrinsic value for him. Whitman believed, whether rightly or wrongly, that this relationship created a situation conducive to the emergence of a newer and richer culture. Of course, the relevance of his achievement could be disputed. Basing their opinion on different assumptions, some radicals and liberals could argue that Whitman's dream for America was moribund. Others, however, may find in Whitman a suggestion for a way to move out of our current cultural wasteland and back into some form of constructive dialogue.

In 1900 the philosopher George Santayana clearly was not

one to look toward Whitman for such help. Santayana believed that Whitman's radical dream for America would never be realized. Although Santayana was attracted to Whitman's vitality and originality but convinced of the poverty of his powers of prescience, his study of Whitman constitutes a strong defense of the humanist against hortatory radicalism. Santayana considered Whitman a spokesman for a breed of "barbarism" that failed to comprehend the increasing complexity and sophistication of modern life.[7] However, at least in appearance, Whitman's ideal state for America prefigures the contemporary world as modern humanists see it. Whitman's dream, in a sense, has become their nightmare. Such humanists have different designations for this trend of American culture. For Trilling, it is "beyond culture." George Steiner calls it "post-cultural," while Ihab Hassan dubs it "post-humanism." Hayden White adopts Erich Auerbach's use of the term "parataxis" to describe contemporary culture. "Paratactical conventions," writes White, "try to resist any impulse to the hierarchical arrangement of images and perceptions, and, as the roots of the word *parataxis* indicate, sanction their 'arrangement side by side'—that is to say indiscriminately, by simple listing in sequence, in what might be called a democracy of lateral coexistence, one next to another."[8] White avers that parataxis describes not only contemporary social reality but also the artistic and intellectual programs of the avant-garde and of radicals. Like other modern humanists, he sees a new coalition of forces fusing to impugn the validity of traditional cultural authority. "Call this new public whatever you wish: pop, youth, body, drug, or nonlinear," White writes, "the fact is that it constitutes a large, rich, and increasingly powerful constituency which shares with the avant-garde artist a distrust of the very category of the artistic and with the utopian radical thinker an indifference to the benefits of historical consciousness as we have cultivated it up to now. This means that by virtue of this new public's dedication to the cult of the casual, the immediate, the transitory, the unstructured, and the aleatory, the avant-garde has an important new ally in its traditional attack upon the critical and custodial operations of the humanities."[9]

Whitman's poetry foreshadows the modern attack on the hierarchical value structure that sustains traditional culture. It subverts what White calls "syntactical strategies" derived from the Greeks "for representing and organizing the experience of the world . . . and for structuring society."[10] Whitman anticipates an avant-garde that, according to White, will not accept "the institution of new privileged positions for old ones—whether of privileged positions in space (as in the old perspectival painting and sculpture), of privileged moments in time (as one finds in the older narrative art of fiction and in conventional historiography), of privileged places in society, of privileged areas in the consciousness (as in the conservative, this is to say, orthodox Freudian psychoanalytic theory), of privileged parts of the body (as the genitally organized sexual lore insists is 'natural'), or privileged positions in culture (on the basis of a presumed superior 'taste'), or in politics (on the basis of presumed superior wisdom)."[11] Of course, to a very real extent, parataxis as it relates to democratic equality is indigenous to the American experience.[12] Inspired by, in Richard Chase's phrase, "a transcendental version of Jeffersonian-Jacksonian democracy," Whitman extended this basic American egalitarian impulse to its extreme—shocking and frightening many of his contemporaries and making his final position pertinent to today.[13]

At the same time, however, in Whitman parataxis functions somewhat differently than it does in modern society as White perceives the society. In Whitman, we get a visible or purposeful parataxis. As a literary device, the paratactical approach misled Santayana into believing that Whitman totally lacked structure. Santayana thought that the desideratum in Whitman "is any principle of selection" to order the "mass of images without structure" and the "abundance of detail without organization."[14] But most critics subsequently have observed that Whitman's poetry, although not most of his prose, exhibits great structure and original organization. His best poetry was the product of a conscious and subtle intention to create the illusion of spontaneity. Whitman clearly was a great and original genius who transformed primitivistic, religious, vernacular, and conventional modes into a highly subtle and structured form of new poetry. As Gay Wilson Allen says, "Whitman was a 'maker' in the literal sense of the term, shaping, experimenting, and revising incessantly until he had achieved a structure in language which satisfied his rational judgment."[15] David Daiches also notes that "structure is of highest importance" in Whitman but then immediately adds that "Whitman's cumulative method also means that his poetry is more open-worked than the kind of poetry which modern criticism is best equipped to handle." In Whitman, he says, "meaning is developed lengthwise, not depthwise; words acquire new meaning by reiteration, and images take on significance by functioning in a series."[16] In other words, Whitman's poetry develops through a form of parataxis.

The paratactical aspect of Whitman's poetry, then, is partly an illusion disguising a solid basis of form and structure. The poetry becomes, in a sense, a major paratactical strategy. It reenforces and sustains other such strategies, all of which vitiate putative positions of privilege as White describes such privilege. But, in contrast to this vision of culture, ensconced within Whitman's paratactical strategies is a deeper commitment. As in all great art, the illusion in Whitman's poetry conveys a deeper truth about life, especially, for Whitman, American life. Thus, inherent in the strategies is the idea of the religious democracy based upon a commitment to culture. For Whitman this meant culture in the full sense of the word—a structure and an atmosphere that allow, instigate, and nourish a dynamic and mutual relationship between common life styles, attitudes, beliefs, and the society's highest ideas and ideals. Implicit in his strategies was a system of beliefs, values, and ideals designed to create and protect the very equality that parataxis represents. They were not instruments of anarchy, but as anticultural strategies they contained their own negation in the ideal of the religious democracy. They operated to keep means and ends consistent. Included within Whitman's overall process of dialectic, the strategies were a concomitant of his version of the Emersonian identity theme involving the relationship of the self with the objective and Transcendental worlds. Thus Whitman, the man of the open road and the bard of the people in all their aspects and experiences, refuses to take that inward turn of the self that enervates the life impulse and vitiates one's bonds with others. He celebrates not an "imperial self" but a joyous and democratic self.

In Whitman's poetry the catalogs are the paratactical foot soldiers in the attack against the list of positions of privilege outlined by White in his essay. The catalogs bring the war to the enemy—privileged time and space, artificial society, restrictive sex, false culture, and even one not on White's list, death. They dramatize Whitman's hatred of social privilege as expressed in *Democratic Vistas* and elsewhere: "Of all dangers to a nation, as things exist in our day, there can be no greater one than having certain portions of the people set off from the rest by a line drawn—they not privileged as others but degraded, humiliated, made of no account."[17] Accordingly, "democracy the leveller," as he calls it in the *Vistas*, is the real hero of the catalog in section 15 of "Song of Myself":

> The bride unrumpled her white dress, the minute-hand of the
>   clock moves slowly,
> The opium-eater reclaims with rigid head and just-open'd lips,
> The prostitute draggles her shawl, her bonnet bobs on her
>   tipsy and pimpled neck,
> The crowd laughs at her blackguard oaths, the men jeer and
>   wink to each other,
> (Miserable! I do not laugh at your oaths nor jeer you!)
> The President holding a cabinet council is surrounded by the
>   great Secretaries,
> On the piazza walk three matrons stately and friendly with
>   twined arms, (p. 35)

Partly through juxtaposition, Whitman establishes an equality between the characters. Helping to connect these images and to relate these apparently disparate individuals is the implied objurgation of the privileged—the comfortable matrons, the pure bride, the remote officials—and the ignorant who allow artificial differences to keep them from recognizing both the universal and the personal elements in others.

Moreover, the technique of the catalog sustains the criticism of the privileged by also attacking, in White's terms, privileged spatial and temporal relationships, as though the acceptance of such structures encourages dehumanizing and antidemocratic impulses. Clearly, Whitman has eliminated traditional time sequence, point of view, and spatial consistency in the catalog to create what Muriel Rukeyser describes as a "film rhythm" in which "the form is montage."[18] Indeed, most modern critics recognize Whitman's attack on traditional syntactical arrangements of privileged time and space. Gay Wilson Allen, for example, writes: "In the mid-nineteenth century all literary compositions that had any standing as literature were constructed on the order of Aristotelian logic: beginning, middle, and end, or in narration, time sequence. Language itself, in fact, is regulated by the laws of syntax, which are but conventions of time and logic. All actions are fitted into the clearly defined categories of 'tense.' . . . But Whitman's 'round house' had no beginning and no end; roundness described . . . the poetic structure with which he was experimenting."[19] Whitman's syntactical revolution relates to what George Steiner in *Language and Silence* calls a general "retreat from the word." Modern poets, according to Steiner, "realized that traditional syntax organizes our perceptions in linear and monistic patterns" and tried to develop new forms that "break out of the traditional confines of syntax and definition."[20] Whitman's poetry contributes to this movement.

In *In Bluebeard's Castle* Steiner goes on to discuss how the alteration of syntactical form in language based on tense indicates new attitudes toward death.[21] Accordingly, Whitman's attack on privileged time and space indicates his attitude toward death, but his feelings about equality placed him in an especially paradoxical position when confronting the issue. Death, the ultimate leveler, was his greatest ally in the fight for equality.[22] Moreover, the sympathy and mourning engendered by death vivified the humanitarian impulse as death does in "When Lilacs Last in the Dooryard Bloom'd." However, death without the promise of new life, as any traditional Christian knows, could be seen as the most pernicious form of tyranny. Death, which was to be welcomed as the leveler of democracy, as the avenue to new life on earth, and as the proof of ultimate spirituality, was less attractive when viewed as the intractable tyrant of the body. Transcendentalism, with its view of life as a double journey of both spiritual and physical dimensions, provided one way out of this dilemma. The other way out was through the body by using the body's own weapon, sex, against the tyrant death.

The work of Norman O. Brown, who sees contemporary paratactical new consciousness at least in part in the form of so-called polymorphous perversity, helps clarify the relationship in Whitman between sexual liberation and death.[23] In his radical interpretation of Freud, Brown maintains that sublimations and sexual repressions give death dominion over life. The resurrection of the body, he says, will occur in this life only by overcoming repressions and sublimations. Once repressions and sublimations are understood as forms of death-in-life, the death and life instincts can become compatible.[24] Brown assumes that the realization that "eternal life can only be life in a body" will enable us to finally reconcile ourselves to ultimate physical destruction.[25] A full life free from death-in-life will enable us to face death willingly. "The death instinct," he writes, "is reconciled with the life instinct only in a life which is not repressed, which leaves no 'unlived lines' in the human body, the death instinct then being affirmed in a body which is willing to die."[26]

Brown's theories help us see that Whitman's "sex program" was designed to raise a new nation of men and women from the realm of the physically dead to a new consciousness in which the victory over death in the body precedes the spiritual victory over the fear of death itself.[27] Anticipating Freud, Whitman stated his conscious insight into the centrality of sex in his famous unforwarded but published letter to Emerson in the 1856 edition of *Leaves of Grass*. In that letter-essay Whitman specifically links sex to immortality as part of a long concatenation of forces and things dependent upon sex: ". . . all existence, all souls, all realization, all decency, all health, all that is worth being here for, all of woman and of man, all beauty, all purity, all sweetness, all friendship, all strength, all life, all immortality."[28] Moreover, in the opening section of the "Children of Adam" poems, Whitman writes of the world transformed into a new garden for the new Adam and Eve who were once physically dead:

> Curious here behold my resurrection after slumber,
> The revolving cycles in their wide sweep having brought me
> again,
> Amorous, mature, all beautiful to me, all wondrous,
> My limbs and the quivering fire that ever plays through them,
> for reasons, most wondrous, (p. 69)

The lines that follow detail the awakening and reviving of the senses in the resurrected body. "Renascent with grossest Nature or among animals," the new Adam and Eve achieve a new humanity which ironically brings them closer to an animal existence, free from human repressions and making them one with nature. "I think I could turn and live with animals, they're so placid and self-contained," Whitman says in section 32 of "Song of Myself." He then lists all the torments which characterize humanity but from which animals are free:

> They do not sweat and whine about their condition,
> They do not lie awake in the dark and weep for their sins,
> They do not make me sick discussing their duty to God,
> Not one is dissatisfied, not one is demented with the mania
> of owning things,
> Not one kneels to another, nor to his kind that lived
> thousands of years ago,
> Not one is respectable or unhappy over the whole earth.
> (p. 47)

Similarly, Norman Brown recommends to traditional psychoanalysis a "body mysticism" not unlike Whitman's mysticism that affirms "the possibility of human perfectibility and the hope of finding a way out of the human neurosis into that simple health that animals enjoy, but not man."[29]

This elevation of what Trilling calls the "authentic" as opposed to the intellectually abstract and artificial involves a journey into the void "beyond culture" as we know it. As Whitman writes in "Song of Myself," "What is known I strip away, / I launch all men and women forward with me into the Unknown" (p. 61). For Brown, our mental health necessitates the break with culture. "Freud's analysis of word-consciousness," he writes, "deepens our understanding, not only of language as neurosis, but also of culture as neurosis and of culture as a 'substitute-gratification,' a provisional arrangement in the quest for real enjoyment."[30] In *Love's Body*, a later work, Brown attempts through an original and paratactical arrangement of brief sections and paragraphs to demonstrate the use of language and the presentation of ideas in a way that goes beyond the so-called repression of conventional forms of language, expression, and argument. Accordingly, Eugene Goodheart writes: "The view of culture as repressive (without the significant qualifications of this view one finds in *Civilization and Its Discontents*) has become the leading motif, so to speak, of recent radical revisionists of psychoanalytic doctrine—like Herbert Marcuse, Norman O. Brown, and R. D. Laing. Under the auspices of psychoanalysis (or of a debased psychoanalysis) the historical ideal of culture as a vehicle of freedom, of the formation of character and mind, has come to be seen as essentially negative."[31]

This journey into the void beyond the word and culture sets a dangerous precedent. To the modern humanist, basic human insecurity fails to abide the unknown for long. Such writers as Goodheart fear that the need for certainty can help turn the utopian impulse into an authoritarian force. Similarly, David Daiches has observed that the paratactical or avant-garde impulse in modern times often occurs with a concomitant commitment to antidemocratic ideas. Daiches believes that modern cultural history indicates that "we can get reactionaries in politics who are revolutionaries in art." He goes on to say, "Politically, then, modernist art is Janus-faced, combining a revolutionary urge to smash the existing system with an ideal vision of order which is often politically reactionary."[32] He argues that such influential modernists as Eliot and Yeats, who sought to smash bourgeoisie attitudes and conventions through their revolutionary art, also believed that democratic commitments tended to cultivate and protect the mediocre. Such avant-gardists searched for new political and cultural forms which would nourish the creative imagination and encourage artistic achievement and superiority. To a certain extent, Whitman's case substantiates fears that modern avant-garde attitudes toward art subvert traditional democratic institutions and help create a situation conducive to the growth of an elitist authoritarianism. Thus, F. O. Matthiessen years ago noted the presence of an inchoate form of fascism in the Transcendentalism of both Whitman and Emerson. However, countering this tendency in Whitman are what Matthiessen and others recognized as deeper concerns and instincts for the "common and humble."[33] These instincts and concerns moved Whitman to espouse a program of religious democracy that obviously distinguishes him from the reactionary proclivity of other artistic and cultural revolutionaries in the paratactical strain. Also, it should be noted that paratactical political programs have cultivated intensely antiauthoritarian movements, not just the reactionary programs of earlier avant-gardists. Like recent paratactical and antiauthoritarian programs that call for greater participation in and democratization of institutions, Whitman also saw the need in his time for the creation of a new culture imbued with the significance of each individual self. He believed that such a culture must be aimed at the elevation of all the people, not just the few. Thus, in "By Blue Ontario's Shore," he writes:

> Have you thought there could be but a single supreme?
> There can be any number of supremes—one does not
>   countervail another any more than one eyesight
>   countervails another, or one life countervails another.
> (p. 241)

Accordingly, Whitman's position on culture as a crucial factor in his democracy puts him much closer to Matthew Arnold than to Yeats or Pound and distinguishes him from Norman O. Brown. In many ways he was, in Richard Chase's phrase, "more 'Arnoldian' than Arnold." "The truth is," writes Chase, "that *Democratic Vistas* is a kind of American version of Arnold's *Culture and Anarchy*."[34] Of course, as Chase indicates, enormous differences separated the two men. But, at the same time, Arnold's "social idea" of culture as a source of inspiration for people of all classes to achieve "sweetness and light" related in many ways to Whitman's own cultural program for religious democracy of spiritually elevated common people. "The men of culture are the true apostles of equality," writes Arnold. "The great men of culture are those who have had a passion for diffusing, for making prevail, for carrying from one end of society to the other, the best knowledge, the best ideas of their time; who have laboured to divest knowledge of all that was harsh, uncouth, difficult, abstract, professional, exclusive; to humanise it, to make it efficient outside the clique of the cultivated and learned, yet still remaining the *best* knowledge and thought of the time, and a true source, therefore, of sweetness and light."[35] Whitman's cultural "programme" in *Democratic Vistas* possessed a similar proselytistic, if also more pedestrian, ring. "I should demand," he says, "a programme of culture, drawn out, not for a single class alone, or for the parlors or lecture rooms, but with an eye to practical life, the west, the workingmen, the facts of farms and jackplanes and engineers, and of the broad range of women also of the middle working strata" (p. 479).

Whitman's emphasis on the importance of culture and education for internalizing independence, self-direction, and free thought as well as his belief, like Thoreau's, in the near religiosity of reading also relate to Arnold's attitudes. Accordingly, both Whitman and Arnold despised what Arnold called "the ordinary popular literature" that tries "to give the masses, as they call them, an intellectual food prepared and adapted in the way they think proper for the actual conditions of the masses."[36] Such literature, Whitman believed, appealed to "the mean flat average," thereby encouraging the mindless conformity that vitiated the Transcendental impulse (p. 488). Both men also saw the danger of the transmogrification of culture into an item for what Veblen calls conspicuous consumption. Whitman carried this concern further than Arnold into an attack on any external cultural influences that would distract the people from developing their own native culture. This hostility to foreign and older cultures, which is qualified by Whitman's recognition of their aesthetic value and their importance in the development of his own career, actually indicates the enormous value he placed upon culture in developing and transmitting democratic ideas.[37] "I say," he writes in the *Vistas*, "that democracy can never prove itself beyond cavil, until it founds and luxuriantly grows its own forms of art, poems, schools, theology, displacing all that exists or that has been produced anywhere in the past under opposite influences" (p. 457). Thus

Whitman like Arnold believed in, to repeat Goodheart's phrase, "the historical ideal of culture as a vehicle of freedom, of the formation of character and mind."

However, the factors in Whitman's "programme" which make it acutely American derive from his attempt to find a structure for continual change. In both *Democratic Vistas* and *The Eighteenth Presidency*, his tract on the 1856 election, Whitman clearly strains to synthesize the two opposing forces of revolution and tradition. In *The Eighteenth Presidency*, he delineates the origins of the cultural tradition which he thought would help create a sense of identity, stability, and purpose for Americans. He cites as a source of authority for American democracy the writings and lives of the founders. "The platforms for the Presidency of These States," he writes, "are simply the organic compacts of The States, the Declaration of Independence, the Federal Constitution, the action of the earlier Congresses, the spirit of the fathers and warriors, the official lives of Washington, Jefferson, Madison, and the now well-understood and morally established rights of man, wherever, the sun shines, the rain falls, and the grass grows."[38] His acceptance of the works and acts of these individuals as a system of belief approaching revealed truth tended to indicate to him that, like the Jews and the Puritans before them, the American people were God's chosen. The Declaration of Independence, he believed, functioned as a contract obligating the American people to set the example for the rest of the world. "This," he says, "is the covenant of the Republic from the beginning, now and forever."[39] He attributed the writing of the Constitution, which was second to the Declaration in "American organic compacts," to "some mighty prophets and gods." He called the document "a perfect and entire thing, an edifice put together, not for a day or year, but for many years, perhaps a thousand, perhaps many thousand."[40] For Whitman, the Constitution—"the greatest piece of moral building ever constructed"—and the other documents became a kind of Bible for the religious democracy. As such they provided a basic stable foundation for the nation. Upon that foundation he wanted to construct a body of written work to explicate, cherish, and protect and fulfill the national "covenant." The burden of the responsibility for leading this culture fell to the poets, who became a similitude to the Hebrew prophets and the Puritan divines, so that their works gained a canonical quality.

Accordingly, much of Whitman's prose, including *Democrat-*

ic Vistas and *The Eighteenth Presidency*, possesses sermonic and jeremiadlike qualities. In both Whitman bitterly castigates those who have failed to honor and perpetuate the tradition of the nation's divinely inspired founders. "Genuine belief," he says in *Democratic Vistas*, "seems to have left us.... We live in an atmosphere of hypocrisy throughout" (p. 461). "Our New World Democracy" he terms "an almost complete failure in its social aspects, and in really grand, religious, moral, literary and aesthetic results" (p. 461). He goes on to call the whole "a sort of dry and flat Sahara" (p. 462). In *The Eighteenth Presidency*, in which Whitman demagogically vilifies political enemies as "pimps" and "body-snatchers" and "sponges" and "pimpled men, scarred inside with the vile disorder," his excessive fulminations are designed to inveigle "the true people" and "the real America" into winning back their nation from corrupt forces, the underlying implication being that this "young genius of America," consisting of its working people, has failed in its duties.[41] In this work, Whitman also calls for the advent of a Redeemer President who will come like the New Messiah of the religious democracy. "Whenever the day comes for him to appear," he writes, "the man who shall be the Redeemer President of These States, is to be the one that fullest realizes the rights of individuals, signified by the impregnable rights of The States, the substratum of this union."[42]

In spite of his loyalty to this tradition, however, as a Jeffersonian Whitman also deified the present and believed in the importance of assuring the self-determination of future generations. He felt that any cultural tradition must remain organically connected to the people it represented and must refrain from becoming an external and alien force in their lives. To vouchsafe the continuation of this organic relationship, he believed that a democratic cultural tradition must also include adequate provision for revolution. "The eager and often inconsiderable appeals of reformers and revolutionists," he says in *Democratic Vistas*, "are indispensable, to counterbalance the inertness and fossilism making so large a part of human institutions. The latter will always take care of themselves—the danger being that they rapidly tend to ossify us. The former is to be treated with indulgence, and even with respect. As circulation to air, so is agitation and a plentiful degree of speculative license to political and moral sanity. Indirectly, but surely, goodness, virtue, law (of the very best), follow freedom. These to democracy, are what the keel is to the ship, or saltness to the ocean" (p. 470). As already noted, Whitman's paratactical strategies—his attacks on privileged forms and structures—performed this revolutionary role in his works. The revolutionary and traditional impulses engaged each other in a dialectical relationship out of which he hoped a newer and healthier cultural environment would emerge.

In *The Eighteenth Presidency* and *Democratic Vistas*, Whitman also seemed to believe that the absence of such a dialectic between revolutionary and traditional liberal forces and ideas enervated the culture's capacity for survival by putting it in the hands of those for whom opposition, negation, and finally democracy itself are anathema. For Whitman, belief in the possibility of cultural progress and relevance through dialectic required a faith somewhat akin to what he felt for the common people—a faith tested for him through the fire of lifelong rejection by the masses. William James, a reader of Whitman who did not reject or dismiss him, discussed this issue of faith in terms that may still be appropriate for our own era, in which palatable alternatives to such faith have failed to materialize for many. "In truths dependent on our personal action," James said, "then, faith based on desire is certainly a lawful and possibly an indispensable thing."[43]

🎵 Chapter 5
Howells: The rebel in the
one-dimensional age

One of the first major American novels in the new realism to relate in a vital and prophetic way the phenomenon of "the perverted self" to basic changes in the social, cultural, and economic structure of late nineteenth-century America is William Dean Howells' *A Modern Instance* (1882). In his study of Bartley Hubbard, Howells presents us with an intensely rebellious and highly perverse character. Accordingly, through numerous authorial intrusions into the text of *A Modern Instance*, Howells condemned Bartley's character, behavior, and appearance. With much justification most modern critics also see Bartley as a contemptible person. The most severe critics view him as a kind of synecdoche for the alienated, modern American middle class.[1] However, these repeated attempts to categorize Bartley as the "average" American tend to overlook the complexity of his role in the novel. Rather than symbolizing a rootless and fragmented middle class, Bartley is "the novel's symbol for the outlaw in life."[2] But he is also more than a mere outlaw. A born rebel, he symbolizes the rebellion of the perverted self. Often without intending it, Bartley finds himself challenging the middle class and its values, standards, and power structure. His problem really is that he has no substantial values or standards to substitute for those he rejects. He is a rebel without a cause, an alien in a materialistic and pretentious society, a precursor of the kind of social dropout that blossomed in this century in the counterculture. His proclivity for self-destruction emphasizes his sense of perversion, while his perpetual sense of flight both in his personal relationships and in his escape to the West at the end of the novel indicates his perverse understanding of the self and freedom. Both in his study of Bartley and in his later social, economic, and utopian novels, Howells demonstrated the breadth and depth of his understanding of the plight of the individual in modern society. He also evidenced one of the best understandings of his time, and perhaps of our own as well, of the way developments in modern culture and society vitiate the values of individualism and autonomy that formed the basis of his own beliefs. Thus, without justifying or condoning Bartley Hubbard's obvious weaknesses—his self-indulgence, moral laxity, selfishness—we should reassess the significance of his character in the novel and American culture as well as his significance for Howells' literary reputation.

However, prior to such a reassessment more should be said about the problem raised in *A Modern Instance* by Howells' authorial intrusions. Howells intrudes to change the point of view, to generalize about specific character traits, to inform, to judge, and to question motivation. At one point, he describes Bartley as "the bulk" and calls him "corrupt."[3] Also, after Bartley learns that he cannot afford to return to his abandoned wife because his wallet has been stolen, Howells intrudes to say: "Now he could not return; nothing remained for him but the ruin he had chosen" (p. 277). By today's standards these examples of intrusion into the novel, which was written before Henry James' pioneer studies of technique, seem heavy-handed. But, in general, Howells' intrusions tend to be fairly objective. Often they add depth to the characters and complexity to the action. The intrusions frequently operate as a means for establishing aesthetic and moral distance among Bartley, the author, and the reader. This distance gives Howells enough room to provide a sense of balance to Bartley's character and to portray him as a villain with some sympathetic qualities. Early in the novel, Howells' description of Bartley's youth is a demonstration of such balance. The sympathy we feel for Bartley the orphan is qualified immediately by the knowledge that he had also been "pitied" and "petted" (p. 20). A deeper dimension is added to his character when we are told that "when his benefactor proposed to educate him for the ministry, with a view to his final use in missionary work, he revolted" (p. 20). With this statement Howells establishes the pattern of acceptance, rejection, and rebellion that is central to Bartley's character.

As an orphan, Bartley Hubbard grows up outside traditional society and traditional institutions. Through much of the novel, he is a man in search of a home and family. Being the outsider is a source of Bartley's strength and weakness. It contributes to his sense of personal and social irresponsibility, but it also gives him a strong sense of independence and objectivity during crucial moments. In the early part of the book we see Bartley, governed by an understandable desire for sympathy, entering the Gaylord household. Being pampered by the Gaylords and others created a false sense of expectations. He goes to them filled with trepidation because of the incident with Henry Bird. Expecting to be treated as a son, he finds himself treated as "the house nigger." Like a favorite house slave, he has been coddled into a full sense of his own dignity only to be cut off at the height of his expectations. Unfortunately, he discovers that the real trouble is not in his returning Bird's slap but in his taking the Gaylord generosity too far by courting the Squire's daughter.

That Gaylord relishes his power over the young man is apparent as soon as Bartley begins relating the incident. Although acting "involuntarily," the Squire still cannot resist assuming "the attitude of a lawyer cross-questioning a slippery witness" (p. 62). "Any witnesses of the assault?" he asks Bartley, using the legal term that prejudges and condemns (p. 63). At the end of the scene, he even admits his true feelings: "You might go to the devil, for all I cared for you" (p. 66).

These actions, however, awaken the rebelliousness in Bartley's character—he rebounds from his initial humiliation and returns to Gaylord's office. Howells writes that "Bartley believed himself sincere, and there is no question but his defiance was so" (pp. 70–71). The Squire responds to this "defiance" and to Bartley's search "for a further pretext of quarrel" (p. 71) with some confusion. This is evident in both his actions and his words as he describes the situation to his wife. Howells writes of the Squire: "He came into the kitchen, and sat down with his hat on, and taking his chin between his fingers, moved uneasily about on his chair" (p. 72). He admits to his wife, "I don't feel sure of anything," and he goes on to say, "I don't believe he would come back at all, now, and if he did, he wouldn't come back on any equal terms. He'd want to have everything his own way. . . . I saw by the way he began to-night that there wasn't anything to be done with him. It was fight from the word go" (pp. 73–74).

The Squire's response to appeals made later by Marcia for a reconciliation between the two men indicates much about the basis for his attitude toward Bartley. Obviously convinced that Bartley is a selfish scamp, obviously concerned with protecting his daughter, the Squire is also motivated by personal pride and parental possessiveness.[4] "I tell you it's no use, Marcia!" he says. "He wouldn't come if I went to him—." And then adds: "I should have to get down in the dust for nothing. He's a bad fellow, I tell you; and you've got to give him up" (p. 78).

More important here, however, the Squire's reaction to Bartley mirrors the depth of the younger man's own rebelliousness. Bartley may be the evil scamp the Squire describes. But he is also more than that. His unwillingness to placate or negotiate with the Squire demonstrates the intensity of his isolation. He is the outsider, the rebel ready to assert himself even at the cost of personal convenience and success. The Squire comes close to seeing this later in the novel when, in response to a question from Mrs. Gaylord concerning Bartley and Marcia's relationship, the Squire says: "*He's* happened. He just keeps happening right along, I guess" (p. 233). This interpretation also accounts for the significance within the novel of Atherton's remarks about the importance of social order and stability. Bartley's very existence represents a permanent threat to society. By fleeing from a very middle-class marriage and escaping to the outermost reaches of the frontier in Whited Sepulchre, Arizona, where he is eventually killed, Bartley demonstrates a life style in direct antipathy to accepted values.

One of the best examples of Bartley's revolt from middle-class values occurs when he is preparing to make his final departure from Equity. He finds that at this point most of his old friends simply hope to use his plight for their personal gain: "It seemed to him that every soul in Equity was making a clutch at the rapidly diminishing sum of money which Squire Gaylord had enclosed to him, and which was all he had in the world" (p. 99). Bartley desperately needs to sell his horse and cutter. His most promising prospective buyer, knowing Bartley's weak bargaining position, attempts to buy as cheaply as possible. The landlord tries to haggle, but Bartley simply refuses. To all the landlord's fabricated complaints about the colt, Bartley answers cryptically, stoically refusing to compromise or to be further abused and humiliated. "At last the landlord said, 'Well he aint [*sic*] so fast as I supposed.' 'He's not so fast a horse as some,' answered Bartley" (p. 100). Losing his patience, Bartley ridicules the landlord, offers a final price, and then abruptly ends the whole conversation. To the landlord, it is inconceivable that Bartley is actually refusing to bargain, refusing to allow his desperate position to further weaken his own dignity. After the landlord has lost the colt and cutter, he comprehends what has happened and appreciates Bartley. In fact, throughout the novel there is a tendency for characters not really to appreciate Bartley until he has walked out on them. Howells writes that the landlord then "went in-doors with a feeling of admiration for colt and man that bordered on reverence" (p. 101).

Ironically, Bartley's independence and strength, which Marcia finds so attractive, also threaten her control over him. Quarrels often arise when she tries to impose her set of values upon her husband. Evidence of this are their disagreement over the posture to be taken toward the Hallecks, a pretentious and hollow family which Marcia looks up to as a model of social form, and their disagreement over journalism. Marcia wants Bartley to enter the more socially acceptable profession of law. Howells writes: "But at the bottom of her heart, though she enjoyed the brilliancy of Bartley's present life, she did not think his occupation comparable to the law in dignity. . . . She could not shake off the old feeling of degradation . . ." (pp. 142–143). In spite of Marcia, Bartley resists the temptation she presents "to get a clerk's place with some lawyer" (p. 146).

Bartley's involvement in journalism remains crucial to the novel. He works as a writer for the *Chronicle-Abstract*, a newspaper edited by his close friend Ricker, and as an editor for the *Events*, a newspaper operated primarily for commercial profit by Witherby. Ricker and Witherby represent two sides of conventional middle-class morality, both of which are conterminous with the larger ambiguities of the Protestant ethic as it manifested itself in the late nineteenth century. Ricker is the professionally dedicated and socially conscientious journalist, "a newspaper man in every breath" whose "great interest in life was the Chronicle-Abstract, which paid him poorly and worked him hard" (p. 153). Witherby, on the other hand, "believes that the press is a great moral engine, and that it ought to run in the interest of the engineer" (p. 209). The measure of his moral limitations is demonstrated by the facility with which he unites both his religious and his business principles. He tells Bartley that "I hold that the first duty of a public journal is to make money for the owner; all the rest follows naturally" and that "no church can do any good till it's on a paying basis" (p. 155).

Ultimately Bartley refuses to accommodate himself to either man. The incident that serves as the catalyst for his break is his behavior in writing a story that really belonged to another. Indeed, writing the story of a backwoods philosopher named Kinney was professionally and personally unethical. However, the situation that develops from the publication of the "Confessions of an Average American" reveals the full complexity of Bartley's character as well as the complicated nature of his relationship to society. Ricker, who agreed to publish the story, refuses to accept responsibility for his own actions. His reaction to the situation is artificial—he adopts a flatulent, overly emotional, self-righteous attitude toward Bartley. Caught in the dilemma of a morally questionable situation, Ricker rather than Bartley becomes symbolic of his milieu by adopting a morally hypocritical attitude. Equally responsible with Bartley for the publication of the story, Ricker resents having his name associated with it. He emotionally ends his friendship with Bartley, an action which creates the appearance rather than the reality of responsibility. Pompously, he tells Bartley that "the next time we meet, will you do me the favor to cut my acquaintance" (p. 259).

Witherby, like Ricker, uses the publication of the story as a pretext for forcing Bartley to end his association with the *Events*. Witherby has never trusted Bartley. More important, he has never trusted himself with Bartley or, rather, has never trusted his ability to either understand or control Bartley. If Bartley, as so many critics have claimed or implied, was representative of the morality of his time, it is probably with Witherby that he would form his strongest association. Confronted, however, with Witherby's moral hypocrisy, social pretentiousness, and personal cowardice, Bartley feels compelled to strike back. He follows the pattern in his life that began as early as his refusal to bow before the Squire and that continues with his behavior toward Marcia, Ricker, the Hallecks, and Atherton. Responding to Witherby's questions about the publication of the Kinney story, Bartley says: "But don't you put on airs of any sort! I understand your game" (p. 267). Witherby is simply afraid that Bartley will eventually expose the publisher's own "nefarious practices" (p. 267). Essentially an outlaw himself, Witherby is instinctively aware of the threat inherent in Bartley's total alienation from all prescribed moral codes. He calls Bartley "a dangerous person" (p. 267). Bartley then returns the word to Witherby: "I don't think they'd consider *you* a dangerous person in *any* position." Bartley, of course, is absolutely correct in the sense in which he is using the word. Witherby certainly is not dangerous, since he poses no threat to the system. He is the system. He is the human being whose conscience, per-

sonality, and values best exemplify the shape of morality in society. "*You* old thief!" Bartley says to him "good-humoredly, almost
affectionately. 'I *have* a mind to tweak your nose!'" (p. 268).

William M. Gibson has said Bartley is "the type of self-made
man which fascinated and repelled his creator" and suggests he
reappears in another novel as Silas Lapham.[5] In the later Howells
novel, however, we see that the differences between Silas and
Bartley are as interesting as their obvious similarities. Silas makes
the mistake of accepting the system. He believes in his paint.
He wants to be a gentleman with the Coreys at their dinner. He
is entirely too serious about himself. Silas' concern with appearances blinds him to deeper corruptions in society and himself.
Bartley, in contrast, operates in another American tradition. He
would rather keep a light burning for his own individual corruptions, of which admittedly there are many.

Seen in this light as a rebel without a cause, Bartley conforms
to the pattern we have described in American literature and culture as the perverted self. Interestingly, given his rebelliousness
and his subsequent self-affirmation and defeat, Bartley also contains many of the elements of the existential antihero as described
by Ihab Hassan in *Radical Innocence*. Hassan identifies Huckle-
berry Finn, Henry Fleming, and Daisy Miller as "prototypes of
initiation."[6] In each case, Hassan argues, initiation moved closer
to renunciation, while the image of the initiate as rebel merged
with the image of the hero as victim.[7] Also, in each case, the
ambiguities associated with the action of initiation paralleled deeper ambiguities in the culture as a whole. Remembering Bartley's
self-destructive journey across the country, we can repeat for him
what Hassan says of Daisy, who journeyed across the sea: "She
is, in short, a rebel and the price of her rebellion is death."[8]
Bartley's death, like the death of the modern hero, or antihero,
involves no sense of social completion or affirmation. It simply
removes a thorn from the side of an unhappy middle class.

This picture of Bartley Hubbard as a young rebel, a lone chal-
lenger of conventional morality, apparently appealed to at least
two other readers of the novel. Writing to Howells on July 24,
1882, Mark Twain told him: "You didn't intend Bartley for me, but
he *is* me, just the same & I enjoy him to the utmost uttermost
& without a pang. Mrs. Clemens indignantly says he doesn't resem-
ble me—which is all she knows about it." In a letter written
in 1911 to a friend, Howells confided: "... but yesterday I read

[a] great part of *A Modern Instance*, and perceived that I had drawn Bartley Hubbard, the false scoundrel, from myself."[9]

With his analysis of the corruption of Bartley Hubbard, Howells began a lifelong study of the impact of the forces of industrialization, urbanization, and modernization upon the individual and upon personal freedom in the new America. His ability to take the basic issues of individualism and democracy and dramatize them through a confrontation with the changing realities of his culture makes him extremely relevant to our own day and further proves, as many writers have claimed, that Howells was a modern consciousness.[10] A comparison of many of his ideas with those of a contemporary writer such as Herbert Marcuse further proves Howells' perspicacity. In his sensitivity to the dangers confronting the individualistic form of democracy that he espoused, Howells focused his political and social vision on the key issues and themes of his day and dramatized them in a way that makes them meaningful to our own age as seen through the ideas and writings of a thinker as contemporary and immediate as Marcuse.

The obvious differences between Howells and Marcuse at first seem to outweigh any similarities. In addition to their sharply contrasting backgrounds, careers, and intellectual sources, an important historical gap exists between them. Howells writes about the cultural and industrial process transforming the American character during its early stages, while Marcuse describes its machinations during its full maturity.

In spite of these differences, however, both men fall within the purview of an American tradition of moral dissent against popular attitudes and values. Although he was a leader for several decades of the American arts and letters "establishment," Howells' political and economic ideas created considerable consternation among some of his contemporaries. On September 23, 1894, soon after he published the "Letters of an Altrurian Traveller" in *The Cosmopolitan*, the New York *Herald* ran "Poets Become Socialists Too: Howells Champions Socialism." This anonymous article called Howells "the foremost champion of socialism among literary men of the present time."[11] Howells, it said, espoused the "unpopular doctrine" to the "surprise and mystification" of his friends.

Moreover, Howells' developing pessimism over American political and economic life also indicates his contemporaneity. He writes Henry James: "I should hardly like to trust pen and ink with all the audacity of my social ideals; but after fifty years of optimistic content with 'civilization' and its ability to come out all right in the end, I now abhor it, and feel that it is coming out all wrong in the end, unless it bases itself anew on real equality." [12] Howells, like many modern social critics, including Marcuse, believes that hostility to meaningful change helped make all segments of American society responsible for worsening conditions. Howells frequently shows how such conservatism and culpability operate in three areas of American life that also receive considerable attention from Marcuse: the domination of materialistic values, the confusion of true and false needs, and one-dimensional thought. I shall consider the similarity of their views on these three subjects of values, needs, and thought, hoping to indicate in the process other areas in which worthwhile comparisons can be made.

The basis of Marcuse's program of social and cultural reorganization rests on his attempt in *Eros and Civilization* to merge the ideas of Freud and Marx. The idea is not new with Marcuse. As early as 1932, Wilhelm Reich's association of the death principle and psychoanalysis with capitalism and with Marx aroused Freud's criticism. Marcuse, however, believes that since then the new technology has given us the power to reconstruct our relationship with our environment and to redesign a culture based on true freedom and eros. His widely disseminated ideas on this subject have generated extensive discussion in both popular and academic publications.

Marcuse, however, does not rely solely upon Freud and Marx to explain the continuations of "surplus repression." In *One-Dimensional Man* he develops a dynamic metaphor to describe the nature and ideology of modern society. He argues that the new technology, which could be the vehicle for our liberation, now operates as a negative and debasing force by controlling our everyday social, political, and intellectual life through the subversion of independence and autonomy. He writes that we have sold our souls—our potential for liberation and transcendence—to what Karl Jaspers called the technical life-order. Technocracy, according to Marcuse, confuses freedom with abundance and teaches that autonomy and independence are technical impossibilities. "The loss," he writes, "of the economic and political liberties which were the real achievement of the preceding two centuries may seem slight damage in a state capable of making the administered life secure and comfortable. If the individuals are satisfied to the point of happiness with the goods and services handed down to them by the administration, why should they insist on different institutions for a different production of different goods and services?"[13] Unfortunately, material wants lead only to perennial dissatisfaction and gluttony. "This society," he writes, "is obscene in producing and indecently exposing a stifling abundance of wares while depriving its victims abroad of the necessities of life; obscene in stuffing itself and its garbage cans while poisoning and burning the scarce foodstuffs in the fields of its aggression; obscene in the words and smiles of its politicians and entertainers; in its prayers, in its ignorance, and in the wisdom of its kept intellectuals."[14]

Howells presents a similar picture of American values in many of his writings, especially in *The Altrurian Romances*. Although, as Edward Wagenknecht says, the *Romances* are not "the full index of his mind," they do encompass most of the ideas expressed in Howells' economic novels and essays.[15] A New Hampshire resort provides the setting for the most important romance, *A Traveller from Altruria*. Early in the story, Mr. Twelvemough, a popular writer, tells Aristides Homos, his Altrurian guest, "our hotel is a sort of microcosm of the American republic."[16] The hotel—with its working and serving class, its affluent middle- and upper-class guests, and its domination of the surrounding countryside—clearly symbolizes American class stratification and inequality. It further dramatizes a view Howells expresses in the essay "Are We a Plutocracy?" published the same year as the novel. "The tramps," Howells writes, "walk the land like the squalid spectres of the laborers who once tilled it. The miners have swarmed up out of their pits, to starve in the open air. . . . If there is much cold and hunger, the price of food and fuel is yet so high as to afford a margin to the operators in coal and grain and meat."[17]

The hotel as a symbol also suggests the perversion of the American Dream in a new society whose economic system demanded the waste and misuse of both natural and human resources. The strife during the years of Howells' radicalization indicated growing frustration over the seizure of traditional outlets for creative energy and individual choice by morally corrupt powers. Several times in *A Traveller from Altruria*, Reuben Camp tells Homos that new land is unavailable at reasonable prices and that the old land will no longer sustain a family. In "Plutocracy"

Howells writes: "The public domain, where in some sort the poor might have provided for themselves, has been lavished on corporations, and its millions of acres have melted away as if they had been a like area of summer clouds."[18]

The problem, however, as Howells saw it, rested on the fact that neither the lower nor the middle classes felt any sense of moral outrage over injustice great enough to diminish their desire to rise socially and economically. Only Mrs. Camp and Reuben, who live outside the hotel, challenge the system's morality. The workers and guests willingly subvert their moral inclinations before the opportunity to profit from the system. Twelvemough describes the situation when he says of Homos: "I felt it ought to have been self-evident to him that when a commonwealth of 60,000,000 Americans based itself upon the great principle of self-seeking, self-seeking was the best thing, and whatever hardship it seemed to work, it must carry with it unseen blessings in ten-fold measure" (p. 71). The manufacturer, after noting that "the real discontent is with the whole system, with the nature of things," goes on to say that any incentive for real equality among the working class dissipates when "they begin to rise. Then they get rid of it mighty soon. Let a man save something—enough to get a house of his own, and take a boarder or two, and perhaps have a little money at interest—and he sees the matter in another light" (pp. 44, 46).

Howells condemns the insatiable appetite of most Americans for material success in his essay on "Plutocracy." He writes that any wage earner "is ready at the first chance to become a wage-giver, and to prosper as far as he can," because "in his heart, he is as thoroughly a plutocrat as any present millionaire."[19] Howells, as already noted, is especially interesting in this refusal to put excessive blame for the system upon one group of privileged people. They may be foolish and ugly like Mrs. Makely and Mrs. Munger, spoiled like the Dryfoos girls, or mean like Gerrish in *Annie Kilburn*, but they cannot be made to carry the responsibility for the whole society. "In fact," writes Howells, "if we have ceased to be a democracy and have become a plutocracy, it is because the immense majority of the American people have no god before Mammon.... If we have a plutocracy, it may be partly because the rich want it, but it is infinitely more because the poor choose it or allow it."[20] Americans, he writes, have it within their power to change the system through the vote. Similarly, in *A Traveller from Altruria* the banker says of the farmers and workers: "They can make any law they want, but they prefer to break such laws as we have" (p. 129). In contrast, the community in *Annie Kilburn* votes against Gerrish, but such behavior is exceptional.

It may be that, taken to its extreme, Howells' view of equality becomes fatuous.[21] Howells, however, uses the term in an almost modern existential sense. True equality, he believes, stems from an inner spiritual source potent enough to counter predominating dehumanizing social forces. Partly from the Christian Socialists, he developed the idea of the criminal nature of capitalistic society. But, as Louis J. Budd indicates, probably Tolstoy's ideas of spirituality affected Howells most powerfully.[22] Like Tolstoy's, Howells' idea of equality requires that we look within ourselves to develop our instincts for goodness and equality. "We shall not have fraternity, human brotherhood," Howells writes in 1896, "without trying for it. From nature it did not come; it came from the heart of man, who in the midst of nature is above it."[23] Society, he believes, enervates one's naturally warm and brotherly instinct. "Social equality," Howells writes, "is the expression of an instinct implanted in us from the first, as we see in children, who, until they are depraved by their elders, have no conception of social differences."[24]

Agreeing on the baseness of dominant American values, Howells and Marcuse also share a recognition of some of the techniques the society uses to perpetuate these values. The technocracy, Marcuse believes, uses its enormous capacity for production and communication to create false consumer needs. These false needs tend to arouse among consumers a false sense of dependence that engages their loyalty. Marcuse writes:

> We may distinguish both true and false needs. "False" are those which are superimposed upon the individual by particular social interests in his repression: the needs which perpetuate toil, aggressiveness, misery and injustice. Their satisfaction might be most gratifying to the individual, but this happiness is not a condition which has to be maintained and protected if it serves to arrest the development of the ability (his own and others) to recognize the disease of the whole and grasp the chances of curing the disease. The result then is euphoria in unhappiness. Most of the prevailing needs to

relax, to have fun, to behave and consume in accordance
with the advertisements, to love and hate what others love
and hate, belong to this category of false needs.[25]

Howells in many ways anticipated this distinction between
real and false needs. An unqualified supporter of the work of
Thorstein Veblen, Howells helped establish the sociologist's reputation by introducing and interpreting his ideas to wider, popular
audiences.[26] This relationship indicates Howells' understanding
of and sympathy for Veblen's epochal insights into American values. Moreover, Howells examines the social and economic problems in his novels through the perspective of the anxious affluent,
the group in which false needs most obviously operate. Howells,
as Jay Martin says, "is chiefly concerned with the degrading effects
of competitive capitalism upon the upper and middle classes."[27]
In his essays "Equality as the Basis of Good Society" and "Who
Are Our Brethren?" Howells indicates that a confusion between
human nature and social conditions creates false needs. "It seems
to me," he writes, "that we are always mistaking our conditions
for our natures, and saying that human nature is greedy and mean
and false and cruel, when only its conditions are so."[28] As early
as *The Rise of Silas Lapham*, Howells demonstrated the difference
between false and true needs. The strength of the Lapham girls
derives from their ability to make such distinctions. In *A Hazard
of New Fortunes* Beaton and the Dryfoos girls embody false needs,
while Fulkerson consciously tries to manipulate public needs to
market *Every Other Week*. In contrast, Lindau gets to the heart
of essential needs when he returns to the slums because he "was
beginning to forget the boor."[29] Interestingly, false needs so effectively alter the Dryfoos family that a return to a simple farm
life proves unthinkable. Toward the end of the novel, March addresses himself directly to this problem of false needs and tastes:
"But conditions *make* character; and people are greedy and foolish, and wish to have and to shine, because having and shining
are held up to them by civilization as the chief good of life."[30]
The Altrurian Romances serve almost as a guidebook to making
these kinds of distinctions between true and false needs.

For Howells and Marcuse the inculcation of false needs vitiates the boundary between the self and the society. Emotional
dependence upon the satisfaction of these needs results finally
in what Marcuse calls one-dimensional thought. The "transplanta-

tion" of social values provides the process for the development of such thought. He writes:

> Indeed, in the most highly developed areas of contemporary society, the transplantation of social into individual needs is so effective that the difference between them seems to be purely theoretical. Can one really distinguish between the mass media as instruments of information and entertainment, and as agents of manipulation and indoctrination? Between the automobile as nuisance and as convenience? Between the horrors and the comforts of functional architecture? Between the work for national defense and the work for corporate gain? Between the private pleasure and the commercial and political utility involved in increasing the birth rate?[31]

To Marcuse the confusion over "the private pleasure and the commercial and political utility" of that pleasure on the level of social, political, and economic action operates on an intellectual level in the form of one-dimensional thought. Feeling totally dependent upon the society, individuals in both their private and public deliberations tend to think in terms conducive to the perpetuation of that society. Public language becomes, again in Karl Jaspers' phrase, the "language of mystification," and thought exhibits the ambience of a false consciousness in which ideas and feelings lose their personal and autonomous authenticity. One-dimensional thought becomes the means for the rationalization of a society that transforms all negations and opposing reality into turbid affirmations. Marcuse says the omnipresent communications, production, and transportation networks of the society

> carry with them prescribed attitudes and habits, certain intellectual and emotional reactions which bind the consumers more or less pleasantly to the producers and, through the latter, to the whole. The products indoctrinate and manipulate; they promote a false consciousness which is immune against its falsehood. And as these beneficial products become available to more social classes, the indoctrination they carry ceases to be publicity; it becomes a way of life. It is a good way of life—much better than before—and as a good way of life, it militates against qualitative change. Thus emerges a pattern of *one-dimensional thought and behavior* in which ideas, aspirations, and objectives that, by their content, tran-

scend the established universe of discourse and action are either repelled or reduced to terms of this universe. They are redefined by the rationality of the given system and of its quantitative extension.[32]

Howells' *A Traveller from Altruria* dramatizes such one-dimensional thought and behavior. At one point Mrs. Makely genuinely shocks Homos, who asks her: "'Do you really think Christ meant that you *ought* always to have the poor with you?' 'Why of course!' she answered triumphantly. 'How else are the sympathies of the rich to be cultivated? The poverty of some and the wealth of others, isn't that what forms the great ties of human brotherhood?'" (p. 88). Beneath the humor of this exchange is a clear example of the kind of one-dimensional thought that occurs throughout the book. Mrs. Makely's justification of poverty was only the most extreme indication of the way most Americans in the story rejected or reduced challenging ideas. Other examples of this kind of thinking are the belief that Americans do not legislate morality in spite of everyday instances to the reverse (p. 22); the pride in suicidal overwork (p. 29); the reduction of Emerson to a "prophet" of business (p. 34); the belief in the superior social position of the American working class (p. 37); the imposition upon nature of humanly contrived values about the survival of the fittest (p. 48); the justification of poverty as an incentive for self-improvement and work (p. 50); the justification of leisure as work (p. 63); the rationalization that slavery was harder on the masters than on the slaves (p. 68); the self-validating argument that whatever most people are doing is right (p. 71); the belief that poverty results only from irresponsibility (p. 81); the idea that individuality is possible without the means to support it (p. 94); the double standard of justice (p. 101); the equation of the poor with the sick and the insane (p. 113); the self-serving argument that business is business (p. 116); the glorification of the wealthy solely because of their wealth (p. 120); and the belief that money can even buy goodness (p. 136).

Among the clique of Twelvemough's friends, these assumptions are discussed and examined in a way that conforms to the pattern of one-dimensional thought. The conversations are a form of entertainment in which none of the participants feels challenged. None seriously considers alternatives or envisions a new dimension of reality for themselves. Suggestions for alternative life styles and more humane economic and political systems are reduced either to a joke, as when the manufacturer discusses his union problems, or to a fantasy, as when the banker discusses a working-class or socialist victory at the polls (pp. 45–46, 128–129). Equally important, the life style and background of these characters and the setting for their conversations at a luxurious hotel provide almost a working model of the elements necessary for the growth of one-dimensionality.

It is interesting that in this novel Howells felt compelled to move out of conventional realism and into utopian fantasy in order to find a perspective free enough from contemporary prejudices to criticize modern society. In *A Hazard of New Fortunes* Conrad Dryfoos and Lindau each operate as a moral consciousness critical of putative values. But, in *The Altrurian Romances*, Altruria itself functions as a moral consciousness.[33] This use of Altruria by Howells becomes even more apparent in the "Letters of an Altrurian Traveller," in which "the old American life, the old American ideals, the old American principles," and "the old American instincts" are discussed (pp. 190, 191). The search for the old America and the true America serves the further purpose of dramatizing the vitiation by one-dimensional thought of a true historical consciousness. The historical naïveté of most Americans continually confounds the Altrurian, while the banker's interpretation of the history of social equality and the Declaration of Independence effectively illustrates the perversion of the past for purposes of justifying the present (pp. 40, 118). On this subject Marcuse writes:

> The functional language is a radically anti-historical language: operational rationality has little room and little use for historical reason. Is this fight against history part of the fight against a dimension of the mind in which centrifugal faculties and forces might develop—faculties and forces that might hinder the total coordination of the individual with the society? Remembrance of the past may give rise to dangerous insights, and the established society seems to be apprehensive of the subversive contents of memory. Remembrance is a mode of dissociation from the given facts, a mode of "mediation" which breaks for short moments, the omnipresent power of the given facts.[34]

For Marcuse tolerance, like history, is perverted to sustain one-dimensional thought. He argues that contemporary conditions have made the liberal rationale for "pure tolerance" irrelevant. In the one-dimensional society, he says, tolerance "serves the protection and preservation of a repressive society" while functioning as a safety valve for the release, dilution, and eventual repression and rejection of ideas dangerous to itself.[35]

In *A Traveller from Altruria*, Howells also demonstrates how tolerance becomes an instrument of self-serving, one-dimensional thought. The treatment Homos receives from the hotel guests presents an example of such behavior and thought. The comfortable patrons accept him as an entertaining addition to the hotel. They welcome rather than ostracize him. He becomes part of the society because its members refuse to allow him or his ideas to represent a challenge to their way of life. At one point Twelvemough seems to penetrate the situation: "I glanced at the Altrurian sitting attentive and silent, and a sudden misgiving crossed my mind concerning him. Was he merely a sort of spiritual solvent, sent for the moment to precipitate whatever sincerity there was in us, and show us what the truth was concerning our relations to each other?" (p. 99). However, in characteristic one-dimensional mass media fashion, Twelvemough immediately turns such an imposing idea into something of use and entertainment. He presents us with a classic example of one-dimensional co-optation as he considers using his idea about Homos "in some sort of purely romantic design" for one of his own popular stories. "I was professionally grateful for it," he adds (p. 99).

In the important speech scene at the end of the novel, Howells presents an even stronger example of one-dimensional tolerance and co-optation. He achieves a highly ironic effect when the audience manages to both accept and disregard Homos' ideas. The speech, which was sponsored, supported, and attended by society, represents the Altrurian's most heroic effort to proffer a new dimension of reality to the Americans. Mrs. Makely even cheers the speech while depersonalizing its contents so completely as to make them impotent. Her cheers, the professor's skepticism, and the workers' reaction result in the same thing—rejection.

The reaction of the workers to Homos and his speech holds a special place in the novel. They grow enthusiastic, and their spokesman Reuben Camp says: "Have Altruria right here, and right now!" (p. 177). For a moment the sympathetic workers seem to overcome one-dimensional thought. But the anticlimactic ending denies Reuben the fulfillment of his expectations and denies the workers any chance for the satisfaction of their hopes. After his speech the Altrurian leaves and eventually disappears among the people in the country and factory towns. His dream for America disappears with him.

To counter what he considers to be the "repressive tolerance" of the majority, Marcuse has proposed a doctrine of "discriminatory tolerance" involving "intolerance against movements from the Right, and toleration of movements from the Left."[36] He sees this as the only solution to what he calls the "absurd situation" of democracy: "The established democracy still provides the only legitimate framework for change and must therefore be defended against all attempts on the Right and the Center to restrict this framework, but at the same time, preservation of the established democracy preserves the *status quo* and the containment of change."[37] This same dilemma appears in *A Traveller from Altruria*. Howells, of course, never found a satisfactory solution to the problem of encouraging change and mitigating injustice within the framework of one-dimensional democracy. When he elaborated upon his utopia in *Through the Eye of the Needle*, this tension remained in a manner which gives that work special relevance today. On the one hand, Howells, like other utopian writers, anticipated the possibility of reorganizing modern society along lines that would make people happy and free. His utopian vision receives new credence from Marcuse's cogent insistence that the potential of modern technology dates Freud's belief in the social need for extensive repression.[38]

On the other hand, however, Howells' utopia also illustrates another side of the utopian dream that relates to Marcuse's concern for intolerance. Howells found that the implementation of his utopian vision in Altruria still required some structure for the facilitation of order. Based upon legislated morality, Altruria included discomforting dystopian elements of social control that placed limits upon freedom, diversity, and individuality. Howells' awareness of this failure to delineate a completely satisfactory alternative to the one-dimensional society caused him some anxiety. In a letter to Charles Eliot Norton, he noted that *Through the Eye of the Needle* contained "confessions of imperfections even in Utopia."[39] He went on to tell Norton that "other dreamers of such dreams have had nothing but pleasure in them; I have had touches of nightmare." Howells' experience with his imaginary utopia might benefit Marcuse, who could visit Altruria through the eye of the needle to examine a society where the practice of discriminatory tolerance became almost a science.

🎗 Chapter 6
Inner death and freedom
in Henry James

In the fictional world of Henry James, the realm of the inner self often becomes a place of retreat, a domain within which the individual may feel safe from danger similar to the "inner citadel" of "the perverted self." Thus, in a recent essay Daniel J. Schneider finds in James a body of work given to analysis in the terms of R. D. Laing's *The Divided Self*. As we saw about Poe, Schneider finds in James "a picture of a self deeply threatened by the world." [1] However, James also relates this realm of the inner self to the attempt of the individual to achieve freedom through experience and through the growth of the so-called moral sense as an informing and developing consciousness. In Henry James, as in the earlier Puritan experience, the way out of the self goes through the self. A strengthened sense of self involves the capacity to escape the self. Thus the inner self can be a place of inner death, as symbolized by the house in the 1881 *Washington Square*, or it can serve as a potential source of energy and creative power, as it does at least to some extent for Isabel Archer in *The Portrait of a Lady*, published in the same year.[2] As Schneider indicates, most of James' major characters experience one of many complicated variations of the self in retreat. However, this threatened self may be retreating from its own experience with the world and its attempt to encounter and deal with this world. What Lionel Trilling calls the tragedy in James stems in part from this paradox of the self seeking its own identity and its freedom. Ironically, the very complexity and ambiguity of reality in its relationship to the moral consciousness could constitute a program for the individual's defeat. Thus, James dramatizes the relationship in all its complexity and ambiguity of the inner self and of moral consciousness as they interact with a threatening, changing, and complicated world.

Many critics at one time concentrated primarily upon the drama and the life of consciousness in its various forms in James' novels. In James the belief in and the search for consciousness have become in themselves a form of religious sensibility.[3] Of course, James' contribution to our understanding of consciousness, freedom, and identity makes him one of the few American writers who in fact actually helped originate—through both his fiction and his criticism—what we have called literary modernism. However, he also evinced a special perspicacity in his understanding of the social, political, and cultural conditions of his time. His understanding of his time has received increased recognition among critics. As William Veeder says, "Today few critics still support the Brooks-Parrington thesis that Henry James was an ivory tower émigré aloof from the turmoil of his times. More and more we realize that James in his development and fiction—and especially in his early development and fiction—experienced the same struggles as the writers whose work he knew well."[4] Thus, it should not come as a surprise that, while James anticipates what Ihab Hassan calls our current age of terror in *The Princess Casamassima* (1886), his first novel of the same year, *The Bostonians*, and his later novel, *What Maisie Knew* (1897), predict and delineate the psychological counterpart to political assassination in the form of the destruction of the self through a false sexual liberation.

In both *The Bostonians* and *The Princess Casamassima* James concerned himself more than in any other of his novels with actual political questions and with the examination of social questions. About *The Bostonians* he writes, "At any rate, the subject is very national, very typical. I wished to write a very *American* tale, a tale characteristic of our social conditions, and I asked myself what was the most salient and peculiar point in our social life. The answer was: the situation of women, the decline of the sentiment of sex, the agitation on their behalf."[5] About the origins of *The Princess Casamassima*, he writes in his preface that "this fiction proceeded directly during the first year of a long residence in London, from the habit and the interest of walking the streets."[6] It is clear that in writing these novels about such subjects James was at least partially concerned about advancing his career and reputation. In fact, in writing *The Princess Casamassima* he was immediately influenced by the poor reception of *The Bostonians*.[7] Thus, in a letter to his brother William, he writes, *"The Princess* will, I trust, appear more 'popular.' I fear *The Bostonians* will be, as a finished work, a fiasco, as not a word, echo or comment on the serial (save your remarks) have come to me (since the row about the first number) from any quarter whatever. The deathly silence seems to indicate that it has fallen flat."[8] Over two years later he confessed to William Dean Howells, his great friend, that "I have entered upon evil days" because of the "injury wrought" upon him "by my two last novels, the *Bostonians* and the *Princess*, from which I expected so much and derived so little. They have reduced the desire, and the demand, for my productions to zero."[9]

In these novels, including *What Maisie Knew*, the impact of social and cultural forces upon the individual self receives special dramatization through the victimization of an innocent consciousness. Thus, in his discussion of Hyacinth Robinson in *The Princess Casamassima*, Trilling writes that "the intention is not to show him as unmanly but as too young to make the claims of maturity; he is the child of the book, always the very youngest person."[10] Similarly, in *The Bostonians* Verena Tarrant functions as a child-woman with conflicting sets of loyalties to people who compete for her affection. Both characters anticipate Maisie, who in some ways seems full-grown in her childhood while being permanently condemned to a form of emotional and psychological impoverishment. The innocence of these characters, it seems to me, cannot be adequately described by Frederick Hoffman's term as "dogmatic" or even by Hassan's image as "radical." They represent a highly complex form of innocence based on James' own complex theory of life and art and fiction. As J. A. Ward indicates, James' use of such protagonists helps him in scenes and situations that are "deliberately ambiguous" to dramatize the mystery and wonder of life.[11] For James the courage to face the condition of ambiguity and to persist in the exploration for truth becomes an exercise in freedom.[12]

Accordingly, the innocent consciousness not only dramatizes the invidiousness of external conditions but also creates a kind of free internal space for the exercise of a free consciousness over these conditions. The impact of the interplay among this consciousness and the external environment and the moral sense fascinates James as part of a process of creativity and freedom. Clearly, many readers then and in our own time misread James because he presents more than a conventional economic and sociological understanding of freedom. Instead, he sees freedom in terms of a deeper American tradition with which his father was personally familiar through Emerson, in which artistic consciousness and creativity could not be separated from the concept of freedom and the autonomous self.[13]

The connection in James involving intelligence, moral sensitivity, art, social reality, and freedom constitutes what Lionel Trilling defines as James' "moral realism." In a famous section of his essay "The Art of Fiction," James discusses an important aspect of this relationship. "There is," he writes, "one point at which the moral sense and the artistic sense lie very near together; that is in the light of the very obvious truth that the deepest quality of a work of art will always be the quality of the mind of the producer. In proportion as that intelligence is fine will the novel, the picture, the statue partake of the substance of beauty and truth."[14] The way in which James saw the relationship of mind, creative intelligence, and freedom is discussed further in his letter to the Deerfield Summer School, which had invited him to lecture on the novel. Maintaining that "the field is vast for freedom, for study, for observation, for satire, for truth," James goes on to say, "I have only two little words for the matter remotely approaching to rule or doctrine; one is life and the other freedom. Tell the ladies and gentlemen, the ingenious inquirers, to consider life directly and closely, and not to be put off with mean and puerile falsities, and be conscientious about it. It is infinitely large, various and comprehensive. Every sort of mind will find what it looks for in it, whereby the novel becomes truly multifarious and illustrative. That is what I mean by liberty; give it its head and let it range."[15] As he grew older and looked back upon his achievements, James felt even more strongly about the connection between a work's moral sense and the intensity of experience and freedom involved in its creation. Thus, in his preface to *The Portrait of a Lady*, he writes "of the perfect dependence of the 'moral' sense of a work of art on the amount of felt life concerned in producing it. The question," he continues, "comes back thus, obviously, to the kind and degree of the artist's prime sensibility, which is the soil out of which his subject springs. The quality and capacity of that soil, its ability to 'grow' with due freshness and straightness any vision of life, represents, strongly or weakly, the projected morality."[16]

According to Trilling this conception of the interconnectedness of reality, freedom, and moral consciousness runs counter to dominant trends in American culture for at least the past century. Critics and cultural historians, Trilling argues, have gone along with an American tendency to divorce reality from mind. "But with us," he writes, "it is always a little too late for mind, yet never too late for honest stupidity; always a little too late for understanding, never too late for righteous, bewildered wrath; always too late for thought, never too late for naive moralizing. We seem to like to condemn our finest but not our worst qualities by pitting them against the exigency of time."[17] While suspicious of James' real commitment to democracy "because his work shows so many of the electric qualities of mind," most traditionally liberal critics, Trilling says, are not "wholly blind to James's great gifts, or even to the grandiose moral intention of these gifts." "But," he continues, "by liberal critics James is traditionally put to the ultimate question: of what use, of what actual political use, are his gifts and their intention? . . . of what possible practical value in our world of impending disaster can James's work be? And James's style, his characters, his subjects, and even his own social origin and the manner of his personal life are adduced to show that his work cannot endure the question."[18]

Thus, for Trilling those critics who tend to feel most uncomfortable with James also tend to be those who often have narrowly defined political and social ideas of reality and fiction. James in contrast to such critics emphasizes that the impoverishment of any one of the aesthetic, political, and moral realms necessarily diminishes the others. For James the challenge to open one's self to all these areas requires the kind of continual reexamination that precludes the rendering of a stifling allegiance to just one. His view of reality, therefore, resembles his brother's philosophy of pragmatism and is consistent with the conception of the pluralistic nature of experience and with the belief in the potential for human growth and freedom.[19] Accordingly, this vision of reality that he presents has even greater relevance today because of its inherent antagonism toward the kind of one-dimensional thought that Herbert Marcuse believes most aptly characterizes our contemporary cultural situation. The commitment to free thought and the creative imagination that constitute the core of James' "moral realism" are sources of strength in any battle against mass thought. Certainly, in *The Bostonians* James not only anticipates the rise of mass culture and media but also offers a cogent study of its potential for vitiating individual freedom. In *The Princess Casamassima* and *The Bostonians* the rise of the public sphere diminishes the private and free self, while in *What Maisie Knew* we see how cultural corruption can make the inner self a place of darkness. In all three novels James describes the trend of a public consciousness that tends to corrupt the inner "soil" of the self.

In a sense all three novels are prison stories that focus on attempts to free innocent captives as much from prejudice and mental and moral stagnation as from constricting physical circumstances.[20] For James freedom for his characters relates to their attempt to exercise their right to contribute through their personal lives and experience to the world's moral imagination. Thus, in Gordon Pirie's interpretation of *The Bostonians* the novel becomes a story of "rescues," even though Verena is not "as conscious of her prison as most distressed heroines are."[21] In a greater sense, however, the whole culture stands in danger of turning into a form of prison symbolized by the repressive nature of both Olive Chancellor's and Basil Ransom's love and by the rise of the power of mass media and mass culture in the form of Matthias Pardon.[22] Considering not only her relationship to the people who are closest to her but also her developing position as a public person with an extremely vulnerable sense of privacy and sense of inner self, Verena could serve as a case study of a mind fighting for its moral and intellectual survival in a new cultural world of publicity, mass media, and public domination.[23]

Unfortunately, the person who poses as Verena's rescuer himself represents a dead culture, the South. He functions in the novel, however, as a symbol not of the dead past but of the future death of American culture.[24] Verena's tears, therefore, at the end of the novel not only predict her sense of her future with Basil Ransom but also indicate the future of the country as well. The ransom, so to speak, has been extremely high. "But though she was glad, he presently discovered that, beneath her hood, she was in tears. It is to be feared that with the union, so far from brilliant, into which she was about to enter, these were not the last she was destined to shed."[25]

The obvious sense of defeat and disappointment in this sad rescue further indicates that the sexual problem in *The Bostonians* really symbolizes the degeneration of the "union"—both national and sexual—into a death culture. The basic fear of freedom, love, life, and imagination that so dominates this novel through so many of its figures of both sexes resounds, as Alfred Habegger says, in Ransom's use of "one of his favorite exclamations . . . 'Murder!'"[26] Readers, therefore, who dislike this novel because they see it as an unfair portrait of the women's movement miss the point, I think, of its accuracy about the culture as a whole. In a culture of death that substitutes mass psychology for moral consciousness, liberation can become only another form of ideological thought designed to further stultify the individual and moral imagination. In such a culture there are no rescuers, and the brave knight turns into an even stronger and even more vicious oppressor.

Similarly, in *The Princess Casamassima* Hyacinth Robinson's search for freedom continually uncovers new prisons. His exciting progression of new awakenings all lead into deeper darkness. His rescuer here in the form of the Princess functions ineptly in a way that ultimately leads him to suicide. For Hyacinth there was first the prison of the conditions surrounding his birth as the illegitimate son of a noble who abandons Hyacinth's mother and is murdered by her. Indeed, one of Hyacinth's first memories involves his visit to his mother's prison cell during her dying moments. In a sense James' image early in the novel of "the mother who bore him" who "was alive in that huge dark tomb" of a prison dominates much of the novel and becomes something of a controlling metaphor for Hyacinth.[27] As with Maisie, Hyacinth will nurture a secret inner self that will struggle unsuccessfully to break free but instead he will find, like his mother, a form of living death.

Later in *The Princess Casamassima* there is a similar scene that represents in a psychological and moral sense a further development of the moment of living death and imprisonment Hyacinth remembers with his mother. In the later scene Hyacinth reflects upon the sadness of the life of the woman, a dressmaker named Miss Pynsent—Pinnie—who had adopted him. James writes, "At the thought of her limited, stinted life, the patient humdrum effort of her needle and scissors, which had ended only in a showroom where there was nothing to show and a pensive reference to the cut of sleeves no longer worn, the tears again rose to his eyes" (p. 302). He later ponders upon his enormous debt to her and again the images that crowd his mind are of deprivation. "He had thought," writes James, "of many things while he sat with Pinnie watching the shadows made by the nightlamp—high, imposing shadows of objects low and mean—and among them he had followed with an imagination that went further in that direction than ever before the probable consequences of his not having been adopted in his babyhood by the dressmaker. The workhouse and the gutter, ignorance and cold, filth and tatters, nights of huddling under bridges and in doorways, vermin, starvation and blows, possibly even the vigorous efflorescence of an inherited disposition to crime—these things, which he saw with unprecedented vividness, suggested themselves as his natural portion" (pp. 313–314).

In spite of such poverty and the portents of even further deprivation, the greater pain for Hyacinth really comes from the opening onto his consciousness of a world of experience from which he has been excluded. The desire to break free from the prison of his limitations fires him. The excitement and the possibility of the city stimulate him. From watching the theater of the streets he moves through his imagination to entertain the possibility of growing himself, of becoming a participant instead of a spectator. "It was not so much that he wanted to enjoy as that he wanted to know," writes James, "his desire wasn't to be pampered but to be initiated" (p. 125). Thus, while he observed the life of the city and the weekend activity at Hyde Park, "a tremendous little drama had taken place privately on the stage of his inner consciousness. He wanted to drive in every carriage, to mount on every horse, to feel on his arm the hand of every pretty woman in the place. In the midst of this his sense was vivid that he belonged to the class whom the 'bloated' as they passed didn't so much rest their eyes on for a quarter of a second" (pp. 125–126).

More than any physical pain or actual hunger the private drama "on the stage of his inner consciousness" stirs Hyacinth, creating within him a deeper hunger for the unknown, for possibility, for experience. Unfortunately, like Jay Gatz, a "Mr. Nobody from Nowhere," he becomes something of a parody of what he imagines the full life to be. Thus, we find the word "bloated" repeated in the novel, only the second time it is used against Hyacinth by the Princess, who, in spite of her strong feelings for him, calls him "a bloated little aristocrat" (p. 395). There is, of course, a quality of the fatuous in the self-inflation of, as James says, "a little bastard bookbinder" who becomes a spokesman for the importance of art and official culture (p. 407). "I think," Hyacinth says, "there can't be too many pictures and statues and works of art." He goes on to say, "The more the better, whether people are hungry or not" (p. 350). Later the Princess says of him, "The misery of the people is by no means always on his heart. You tell me what he has told you; well, he has told me that the people may perish over and over rather than the conquests of civilization shall be sacrificed to them" (pp. 395–396).

However, there exists a pathetic dignity about the slightly built Hyacinth which is almost Chaplin-like when juxtaposed against the other characters in the novel. While not quite the artistic consciousness that Trilling claims, there is in Hyacinth the kind of "sincerity" that indicates for James a depth and intensity of character that can lead to true moral consciousness. Compared to his friend Paul Muniment, who thinks of himself as strong and standing for the people but who proves to be largely irrelevant, Hyacinth emerges as the far more complex character capable of a much broader range of experience. Paul in his complacency and arrogance never really extends himself. He waits for the world—the revolution—to come to him while Hyacinth, in the continuing struggle to free himself from his past and his limitations, tends to surpass himself as he takes unexpected turns that lead him to modify his goals.

Hyacinth stands in sharpest contrast, of course, to the Princess, who may be one of modern literature's first examples of a radically chic celebrity. In a sense the difference between them is the difference between an attempt at real art as opposed to a commitment to entertainment. A woman who "sold herself for a title and fortune" (p. 211), she continues to sell herself in a role that she plays with ever increasing intensity. But it is a role in which she never changes, a role in which the mask of self, in the sense of Nietzsche's use of the mask, never alters. "She wants to see dirty hands," Hyacinth says of her, without quite realizing the dehumanizing implication of her need for an exhibition of a cause that turns the poor into objects (p. 162). For example, to win her favor by satisfying this compulsion one friend, Captain Godfrey Sholto, says, to Hyacinth, "The day I saw she was turning her attention to the rising democracy I began to collect little democrats. That's how I collected you" (p. 292). Although she is never quite without some form of luxury and support, her absolute commitment is beyond question. When she says, "I'd give up everything—everything!" (p. 159), she speaks the truth because she needs to surrender herself to an all-consuming force. She needs the people and she needs history. Thus, she follows what Hyacinth sees as this "mysterious longing" to meet and "to know the *people*, and to know them intimately—the toilers and strugglers and sufferers—because she was convinced that they were the most interesting portion of society" (pp. 201, 200). For the Princess, however, such involvement continues her surrender of self, which for James also means a surrender of freedom. This suggests a surrender of responsibility and moral consciousness, and for James such a loss can prove expensive for all involved.

While most of my examples so far of the perverted self turn inward on themselves to escape reality, the Princess reverses the process. She goes outward to avoid the inner source of creativity and examination. Afraid of herself and her freedom, she demands more experience to narcotize herself. As Trilling says, "A perfect drunkard of reality, she is ever drawn to look for stronger and stronger drams. Inevitably, of course, the great irony of her fate is that the more passionately she seeks reality and the happier she becomes in her belief that she is close to it, the further removed she is."[28] Trilling further notes that this situation must lead her from Hyacinth to Paul, with his "absolute morality which gives her permission to devaluate and even destroy all that she has known of human good because it has been connected with her own frivolous, self-betraying past." He then describes her in terms very similar to the idea of the perverted self that we have used in this study: "She cannot but mistake the nature of reality, for she believes it is a thing, a position, a finality, a bedrock. She is, in short, the very embodiment of the modern will which masks itself in virtue, making itself appear harmless, the will that hates itself and finds its manifestations guilty and is able to exist only if it operates in the name of virtue, that despises the variety and modulations of the human story and longs for an absolute humanity, which is but another way of saying a nothingness."[29] While this deadness extends into Hyacinth's life and turns him against himself, he survives in terms of his moral consciousness and human spirit. He realizes, as already noted, a tragic dimension.

In *What Maisie Knew*, however, the question of the survival of the moral sense achieves even greater significance partly because of the growing importance of a form of internal death of the self. The inward turn of *Maisie* signals the lessening likelihood of escape from the prison of the self to a liberation of the moral self capable of engaging pragmatically, freely, and realistically in a pluralistic universe.[30] Thus, the question of the condition of Maisie's moral sense has interested many critics. Since she is the victim of depraved sets of parents who consider the major value of marriage to be the opportunity it affords for adultery, Maisie's innocence seems irreparably soiled to critics leaning toward the Freudian view who emphasize the malignant influence of her parents and stepparents. One such critic carries the sexual interpretation of *Maisie* to the point of seeing the whole novel in those terms.[31] Other critics, however, return from renewed examinations of Maisie's character to find her moral nature as sound as ever.[32] For example, in an article relating the James novel to the Jacobean drama, Martha Banta argues that "the victory of goodness" in *Maisie* placed it "within the larger tradition of Christian comedy."[33]

There is, however, another aspect that disputes this optimistic view of Maisie's powers and future. It is also possible to see *Maisie* in terms of an unsuccessful struggle for life and for love. Thus, James in his preface refers to the "death of her childhood."[34] In this context, he speaks of childhood both in a chronological sense and in a moral sense. At the same time another sense of the "death of her childhood" exists. This involves the idea that her childhood actually represents a form of death, an internal psychological death from which she can never escape. In spite of repeated attempts, she cannot escape this syndrome because of herself and her surroundings. This concept fits into a wider thematic pattern of death and sterility in the novel while also further developing the theme, in such other works as *The Bostonians* and *The Princess Casamassima*, of an inner self as a potential prison and a place of death. In *Maisie* the depraved society of London is a dead world. Sir Claude is a coward before women. Ida Farange is a nymphomaniac apparently incapable of satisfaction. All the characters, including Mrs. Wix, seem unable to give and sustain life.

Throughout the novel, Maisie is like a little girl on a merry-go-round that never stops turning. It runs faster and faster past the faces of the people that she loves but can never quite reach. At one point early in the novel, Maisie begins to realize that she will never get off. Her expectations of happiness, love, and security have been raised by her acquaintance with her governesses, Mrs. Wix and Miss Overmore, but she finds that she cannot hold onto them for very long. Also, she learns that forces beyond her control make it possible that at any moment all the people for whom she has been reaching could disappear. Thus, related to the theme of inner death is the continuing growth of what James calls Maisie's unformulated fatalism. As Mrs. Wix and Miss Overmore argue over her future, "Maisie found in this exchange of asperities a fresh incitement to the unformulated fatalism in which her sense of her own career had long since taken refuge; and it was the beginning for her of a deeper prevision that, in spite of Miss Overmore's brilliancy and Mrs. Wix's passion, she should live to see a change in the nature of the struggle she appeared to have come into the world to produce. It would still be essentially a struggle, but its object would be *not* to receive her."[35]

In the opening paragraph of chapter 1, James anticipates his description of Maisie's unformulated fatalism when he says that "it was to be the fate of this patient little girl to see much more than any little girl, however patient, had perhaps ever understood before" (p. 23). Maisie's proclivity for fatalistic prevision also appears with her awareness of her impending separation from Miss Overmore. Here James talks again of Maisie's fate and then writes: "There was no question at present of Miss Overmore's going back with her; it was universally recognized that her quarrel with Mrs. Farange was much too acute. The child felt it from the first..." (p. 34). It was, in other words, Maisie's fate to be fatalistic, to foresee her future of losses and her destiny of loneliness.

As early as the second chapter, the pattern of Maisie's childhood as a kind of death, and her inner life as a force unable to be born, is firmly established. James describes her at this stage as discovering an inner self that is a vessel of secrecy. The discovery of this inner self comes in response to the danger Maisie sees around her. James writes: "She had a new feeling, the feeling of danger; on which a new remedy rose to meet it, the idea of an inner self, or in other words, of concealment" (p. 28). Maisie's initial concentration on this inner self represents a pragmatic reaction to her environment. She believes that, in order to survive, she must convince people that she is a stupid child. She becomes that stupid child for her parents, and their acceptance of her stupidity gives her the freedom to nourish what she thinks of as the secret self they cannot touch.

Following a pattern in James involving the paradox of the self, this inward turn on Maisie's part seems to produce positive results for a while. The inner self becomes a source of strength. James says that she found "a pleasure new and keen" through her secrecy and that "she saw more and more." However, he quickly adds that "she saw too much" (p. 28). The tragic irony of this retreat into an inner self is that it suggests a retreat from life. For Maisie this inner self becomes the womb of her hopes for a new life. But these hopes are continually disappointed. She continually attempts to create a new life but always the end result is stillborn. Maisie's life takes on a definite pattern of schizo-phrenia as that mental condition has been described by such psychiatrists as Laing and Erikson.

It is Maisie's governesses who help us understand the signi-ficance of this secret womb as a source of both hope and death. James writes: "It was Miss Overmore, her first governess, who on a momentous occasion had sown the seeds of secrecy, sown them not by anything she said, but by a mere roll of those fine eyes which Maisie already admired" (p. 28). James' language and im-agery here may not be sexual, but there certainly is the implica-tion that the idea planted in Maisie will bear fruit. Maisie goes from Miss Overmore to Mrs. Wix, the new governess, and Mrs. Wix becomes a midwife who will deliver dead dreams. James writes of Mrs. Wix that "something in her voice at the end of an hour touched the little girl in a spot that had never even yet been reached" (p. 34). He then tells us that, in Mrs. Wix, Maisie had finally found someone she could think of as a mother.

In the very next sentence, however, we find that Maisie is forced into thinking of her relationship with her new momma not solely in terms of new life but in terms of renewed death as well. Mrs. Wix has a dead daughter. With his incorrigible de-light in extracting humor out of morbidity, James writes of "the little dead Clara Matilda, who, on a crossing in Harrow Road, had been knocked down and crushed by the cruellest of hansoms" (pp. 34–35). Mrs. Wix tells Maisie that "she's your dead little sister" (p. 35). If to some extent Maisie replaces Clara Matilda, it is also true that the dead girl becomes a symbol for Maisie of her own deadness. James writes of Maisie that in "an extra-ordinarily short time she found herself as deeply absorbed in the image of the little dead Clara Matilda . . . as she had ever found herself in the family group made by one of seven" (pp. 34–35). Maisie's compulsive attraction to this dead girl grows: "Maisie knew everything about her that could be known, everything she had said or done in her little mutilated life, exactly how lovely she was, exactly how her hair was curled and her frocks were trimmed" (p. 35). She also thinks of the dead girl in a "roman-tic" sense heightened by the fact that "she wasn't a real sister" at all (p. 35). She also finds that thinking of Clara Matilda is "safe," and it is obvious that she finds the same kind of psychological safety in death that she finds in her retreats into her inner self (p. 36). This connection between Maisie's vision of Clara Matilda as a symbol of her own death and Maisie's sense of her secret inner life as a source of security is made clearer when James tells us that her knowledge of the dead girl must be kept "an unutterable and inexhaustible little secret with Mrs. Wix" (p. 35).

It is only natural that Maisie should think in terms of death, for the world into which she is born is incapable of adequately providing for her. Both her mother and father, Beale and Ida, claim to be unable to financially support their young child. They also cannot support her emotionally. The infant that neither parent really wants is "disposed of in a manner worthy of the judgment-seat of Solomon. She was divided in two and the portions tossed impartially to the disputants" (p. 18). In the opening chapter James talks of Maisie as "a drummer-boy... in the thick of the fight" (p. 23). He describes the situation of her life as a kind of horror show of "strange shadows dancing on a sheet," a show in which there will be a "sacrifice" of the "mite of a half-sacred infant" (p. 23). He goes on to describe Beale Farange throwing Ida's unopened letters to Maisie, "like dangerous missiles," into the fire (p. 24). Although the infant is amused by Beale's performance and enjoys "the charm of the violence," the scene gives one the inescapable feeling that it is Maisie, as well as her mother, who is being cast into the fire. Later in the novel, Ida will tell Maisie: "Your father wishes you were dead—that my dear, is what your father wishes. You'll have to get used to it as I've done— I mean to his wishing that I'm dead" (p. 177).

It is, however, around Sir Claude, Maisie's future stepfather and Miss Overmore's eventual lover, that much of Maisie's fatalism and inner death evolve. Her relationship with Sir Claude becomes an intensification of the relationships she has had with others, for it will turn to nothing. In emotional scenes with her mother and father, Maisie will attempt again to demonstrate real love. Her mother, whose inability to control her emotions grows throughout the novel, will interpret Maisie's gesture of love as an attack and will respond accordingly. Her father will simply treat her authentic expression of love with typical cynical indifference.

Although Sir Claude returns her love to some degree, death still stalks Maisie. Sir Claude, with all his kindness and sincerity, is not the man to help give Maisie real life. There is a touch of effeminacy in his character, and his admitted fear of women makes him basically inept as Maisie's savior. All he does is raise her expectations and then shatter them as soon as they are expressed. In some ways, he replaces Mrs. Wix as the conjurer of Maisie's dead dreams. This is clear toward the end of the novel, when both Maisie and Mrs. Wix wait anxiously for Sir Claude's arrival. Instead of the stepfather, a "free" Mrs. Beale arrives alone. James writes that Maisie "knew his dressing-bag now—oh with the fondest knowledge!—and there was an instant during which its not being there was a stroke of the worst news. She was yet to learn what it could be to recognise in some lapse of a sequence the proof of an extinction, and therefore remained unaware that this momentary pang was a foretaste of the experience of death" (p. 228). Actually, her whole relationship with Sir Claude had this "foretaste of the experience of death." At a point much earlier in the novel, Sir Claude's arrival at her house causes Maisie to look and feel like a duchess (p. 117). The feeling quickly fades, however, as the discussion turns to Sir Claude's broken promises to Maisie.

Later, during a stroll in Kensington Gardens, Sir Claude and Maisie accidentally encounter Maisie's mother with her new lover. This meeting drives Sir Claude into an impotent rage and later indirectly causes his first disharmony with Maisie. Out of a sense of loyalty to her mother, Maisie must be less than honest with Sir Claude. Once again, secrecy and love become mixed in Maisie in a way that assures her the loss of love. Talking to Sir Claude, Maisie "could only face doggedly the ugliness of seeming disagreeable, as she used to face it in the hours when her father, for her blankness, called her a dirty little donkey, and her mother, for her falsity, pushed her out of the room" (p. 131).

At the end of the novel, Maisie discovers that at the heart of Sir Claude's fear of women is the fear of himself. She discovers, in addition, that at the heart of her own fear is a fear of herself. James writes: "Now in truth she felt the coldness of her terror, and it seemed to her that suddenly she knew, as she knew it about Sir Claude, what she was afraid of. She was afraid of herself. She looked at him in such a way that it brought, she could see, wonder into his face, a wonder held in check..." (p. 262). It is interesting to note, then, that if it were fear that was involved in keeping them apart it was also fear that in the beginning drove Maisie into herself. There is the intimation that inspired by her love and need for Sir Claude, and enlightened by her knowledge of her fear, Maisie is capable of defeating this fear. This occurs when she tries to persuade Sir Claude to leave for Paris with her. "She had had a real fright but had fallen back to earth. The odd thing was that in her fall her fear too had been dashed and broken. It was gone" (p. 267). The problem, of course, is that

Sir Claude is incapable of losing his fear. The result for Maisie is what the results of her love have always been. Nothing.

One of the great ironies of James is that, for a writer whose belief in liberty and moral consciousness was so profound, his vision continuously opened onto death and darkness. World events during the last years of his life seemed to follow such a vision. Thus, his reaction to the beginning of the First World War dramatizes the contrast between what he saw for the future of liberty as opposed to what he had hoped for that future. He writes, "The taper went out last night, and I am afraid I now kindle it again to a very feeble ray—for it's vain to try to talk as if one weren't living in a nightmare of the deepest dye. How can what is going on not be to one as a huge horror of blackness? ... The plunge of civilization into this abyss of blood and darkness by the wanton feat of those two infamous autocrats is a thing that so gives away the whole long age during which we have supposed the world to be, with whatever abatement, gradually bettering, that to have to take it all now for what the treacherous years were all the while really making for and *meaning* is too tragic for any words."[36]

♫ Chapter 7

Charles Ives: A modern perversion of transcendentalism

On July 4, 1974, the city of Danbury, Connecticut, celebrated the centennial of the birth of one of its native sons, composer Charles Ives. During the feature concert, which was sold out in advance, an audience of more than ten thousand heard Leonard Bernstein conduct the American Symphony Orchestra in Ives' Second Symphony. On the following day, in the New York *Times*, the writer who covered the celebration described Ives as "the rugged individual who is by general consent the most significant composer produced by this country."[1] The success of the celebration and the reaction in the press indicate the widespread recognition of Ives' contribution to music. However, appreciation of his work and place in the history of music had been growing even before the centennial sparked special enthusiasm for him. During the past ten years, his music has appeared with increasing frequency on concert programs around the country. Moreover, serious students have long acknowledged Ives as the first modern composer to develop such devices as dissonant counterpoint, polychordal and polytonal harmonies, half tones, and the many other elements that comprise the "new music."

An ever wider audience has come to enjoy Ives' highly subjective and original style. In addition, ever since his initial "discovery" in 1927, Ives has been lauded as a man composing authentically American music as opposed to works in the tradition of the European masters. Discussing Ives' Fourth Symphony, Lawrence Gilman in the *Herald-Tribune* on January 31, 1927, wrote: "Mr. Ives is an American, and his symphony is the musical testament of a New Englander.... This music is as indisputably American in impulse and spiritual texture as the prose of Jonathan Edwards."[2] For general audiences what makes Ives seem so American is his use of native and popular materials. For example, in the Second Symphony, the music Ives heard as a boy at camp meetings and at town concerts and events in Connecticut—such as "America the Beautiful," "Columbia the Gem of the Ocean," and "Turkey in the Straw"—is quoted.[3] Also, his reputation as a lonely genius and a brilliant innovator who dared to defy conventional taste and standards in order to create new sounds and new techniques further contributes to the increasing popularity of his public image. On the whole, then, a century after his birth, Charles Ives has become a secure part of the musical establishment that had rejected him throughout most of his life.

At the same time, however, the question of Ives' significance for American culture remains open. A need persists to further discuss Ives as a cultural phenomenon in the way Mark Twain has been studied. In Twain's work and life critics discern a conflict of values concerning vernacular versus conventional modes and pastoral as opposed to progressive or technological attitudes. As with Twain, the life and work of Charles Ives also reflect deeper issues endemic in American culture. As Frank R. Rossiter says, "His artistic misfortunes and contradictions were, after all, more of a reflection on American culture than on the man himself."[4] Writers who have discussed Ives from this standpoint of his meaning for American culture usually concentrate on the conflict between his creative genius and his deep involvement in the insurance business. In fact, however, Ives' ideas and writings are relevant to our study because of the ways in which they exemplify the perversion of the self and of individualism in American culture through the growth of a distorted idealism. Ives seems to embody the process through which the Hegelian "law of the heart" evolves into the perversion of the self. He took the strain of perversion in Transcendentalist thought in its inchoate form and developed it in accordance with his own proclivities, including a tendency to retreat within himself behind a wall of his ideas and ideals.

A prominent, innovative, and financially successful insurance executive, Ives did his most productive and creative composing in his spare time during a twenty-year period from 1896 to 1916. He believed that his separate identity as an insurance man for his own agency and for New York Mutual freed him to compose music untainted by commercial needs. However, David Wooldridge, in a recent study of Ives, sees him as a man emasculated by his wife and deluded by the American dream of financial success.[5] Virgil Thomson, the composer-critic, likewise sees Ives as a man of "two faces," implying that the division of energies and the inevitable conflict between the two worlds of insurance and music were at least partially responsible for the premature demise of Ives' creativity during his middle years, when he should have been most productive. Following his physical collapse in 1918, which resulted in a cardiac disability, "something also happened in his brain" to make further creativity impossible, according to Thomson.[6] By 1927 Ives had essentially retired from the insurance business. He lived until 1954, long enough to see the music of his earlier years acclaimed by the public as well as the experts.

However, in order to gain deeper insight into Ives' significance for American culture, it is necessary to delve into his understanding of American Transcendentalism. As Wooldridge says, Ives had an "absolute commitment to the group of mid 19th century writers and thinkers known as the New England Transcendentalists." Similarly, Rosalie Perry maintains that in Transcendentalism and in the works of Emerson in particular Ives "found sustenance for his life and work."[7] Thus, Ives read deeply into the works of the Transcendentalists and believed they offered the best expression of the native American tradition of democracy and independence. One of his most important piano compositions, the *Concord* Sonata, was written as a kind of tribute to them. The sonata is divided into sections on Emerson, whom he adulated, Hawthorne, the Alcotts, and Thoreau, whose independence he admired. He also wrote a series of essays to accompany this music. Ives felt the need to write *Essays Before a Sonata* because he recognized the difficulty of translating ideas expressed in written language into another medium, music. In the prologue to the *Essays*, he indicates that he composed the music as an expression of his own attitudes toward the Transcendentalists. In this music one can sense the presence of a composer of complete self-confidence who is sure of his own feelings and who places great faith in his own instincts and reactions. The sonata clearly indicates that Ives reacted deeply to the special qualities he saw in each of the Transcendentalists. For Thoreau the music conveys a sense of tension, desire, and isolation, while for the Alcotts lightness and sentimentality predominate. In the controlled dissonance of the Emerson section there are elements of grandness, relentlessness, and adventure, while the Hawthorne piece, as one would expect, creates a feeling of darkness, fear, and conflict mixed with an almost humorous irony.

In the accompanying *Essays*, Ives intended to expand upon these feelings. The *Essays* and the sonata, therefore, are simply two different expressions, approaches, and languages dealing with the same subject—Charles Ives and the Transcendentalists. As Ives' biographers Henry and Sidney Cowell state, "The *Essays* do not explain the music; they demonstrate the mind that made it."[8] Accordingly, it is to the *Essays* and his other written works that we must turn to understand the mind of Charles Ives. Unfortunately, however, in these writings one finds a degree of chaos that must be attributed to more than Ives' uncertainty over working in a medium other than music. Actually, at times Ives could be a fairly strong writer whose use of metaphors and aphorism demonstrates his ability to learn from his readings of the Transcendentalists. Thus, he was capable of writing that Thoreau was "a great musician, not because he played the flute but because he did not have to go to Boston to hear 'the Symphony.'"[9] Also, in his essay on Emerson he compared a home run to achieving a special triumph in music. "A home run," he says, "will cause more unity in the grandstand than in the season's batting average" (p. 23). But these lines are exceptions to his general use of language, which is largely characterized by overstatement, overgeneralization, awkwardness, and even blatant foolishness.

Moreover, such failures in Ives as a writer have deeper significance. They indicate problems in the way he thought. In contrast to his music, which is open, free, and experimental, his writings demonstrate a need to create a closed world of moral absolutes intolerant of ambiguity and uncertainty. Ives created this world out of his understanding of the Transcendentalists. He transmogrified the writings primarily of Emerson and Thoreau into a closed system of ideals and beliefs that could justify all his actions, prejudices, and values. This tendency in his thinking, as evidenced in his interpretation of the Transcendentalists, forms a pattern that is sustained in his attitude toward important writers and thinkers of his own day. As one would expect, Ives was uncomfortable with the major contemporary forces behind realism and pragmatism. As Rossiter says, "Ives's writings indicate that he had little knowledge of the major intellectual currents in America in these years. Figures like William James, Holmes, Dewey, Veblen, and Beard do not seem to have affected his thinking; indeed, the pragmatism and relativism of their work would have been anathema to him."[10]

Accordingly, Ives describes Emerson in the *Essays* as a Promethean savior figure who delivers ultimate truth to humanity. "We see him," Ives writes, "standing on a summit at the door of the infinite, where many men do not care to climb, peering into the mysteries of life, contemplating the eternities, hurling back whatever he discovers there—now thunderbolts for us to grasp, if we can, and translate—now placing quietly, even tenderly, in our hands things that we may see without effort; if we won't see them, so much the worse for us" (p. 12).

The extravagance of this statement and the tone of the *Essays* in general indicate that for Ives Transcendentalism served almost a religious function. It became a way of finding meaning and certainty at a time when the world was still unaccustomed to a new condition of life dominated by perpetual change in all spheres of activity. Significantly, in his other writings on political, social, and business issues, Ives distorts Transcendentalism even more severely. In "The Majority," a long essay delineating his political beliefs, Ives corrupts Emerson's conception of the Over-Soul into the deification of the majority as the literal embodiment of moral truth, political justice, and God's will. He writes: "It must be assumed, in the final analysis and consideration of all social phenomena, that the Majority, right or wrong, are always right" (p. 163). When they act as a majority, he believed humans approach universal consciousness. "God," he says, "is on the side of the Majority" (p. 144). Again speaking for God, Ives adds "that He is not particularly enthusiastic about the Minority, that He has made Men greater than Man, that He has made the Common Heart, the Universal Mind, and the Over-Soul greater than the individual heart, mind and soul, and the predominant part of each" (p. 144). Taken to its extreme, Ives' view of the majority became the elevation of the individual not in his or her uniqueness and originality but in the mass. Espousing "the divine law of averages," Ives finally celebrated "this Majority giant, this great mass personality" (pp. 198, 199).

In his desire to protect the majority against impending incursions by what he called "the hog mind of the Minority," Ives devised an elaborate system for registering majority opinion. In a proposal for an amendment to the Constitution that would allow for the recording of mass opinion on important issues, Ives indicated that modern technology could now make "universal expression" and "direct democracy" possible. In effect, he was trying to recapture his sense of the New England town meeting on a national scale—he was trying to adapt his idea of a dead mythic past to the technology of the modern era. But he failed to recognize the implications of his ideas for democratic government and for minority rights.

Ives also attempted to apply his understanding of Transcendentalism to modern insurance salesmanship and corporate values. In notes, memoranda, and a pamphlet on insurance salesmanship, "The Amount to Carry," Ives proselytized his version of Transcendentalism. Henry and Sidney Cowell, who describe the pamphlet "as a handbook for insurance agents," state that in much of the work "Ives carries forward his instruction on the broadest Transcendental lines, outlining a kind of social history of the concept of insurance."[11] In fact, however, much of the writing demonstrates one man's Transcendentalism reduced to a public relations approach to salesmanship and business efficiency. *"Life insurance is doing its part in the progress of the greater life values,"* Ives emphasizes.[12] Concentrating on sales technique and psychology in the pamphlet, he advises agents on how to overcome "The Prospect's Objections" and suggests in another section on prospects that "If He Debates, Your Hold On Him Is Growing." In one of the many memoranda he sent to his agents, Ives notes, "If you can't make your prospect like you or your policy, make him like Life Insurance anyway. Knock some BIG ideas into his mind. Everyman wants to be independent and have his family independent. That's the spirit of America and of humans in general. Nothing can help a man more than the thing you have for him: Life Insurance."[13]

In spite of the crass materialism and questionable ethics that these sentiments suggest, Ives persisted in his belief that he was inculcating the industry with a higher Transcendental purpose. He convinced himself that insurance was a vital element sustaining the whole structure of a moral universe that he thought was within each person's grasp. In his picture of insurance there was not even room for the known facts concerning the history of corruption in the industry that had been revealed through a series of public scandals and investigations. As Wooldridge says, "It still seems incredible that Charles Ives didn't know what he was getting into. Life insurance by the turn of the century was so corrupt it seems incredible that everybody didn't know it."[14] Ives' capacity for self-delusion also appears in a fifteen-page memorandum to the executives of the Mutual Life Insurance Company. In this memorandum Ives was comfortable justifying even the most platitudinous ideas and ideals in terms of their appeal to economic self-interest and "the apparent advantages to the Company."[15] Giving in to his compulsion to place a moralistic and righteous tinge upon all his activities, he allowed himself to become an apologist for modern corporate values and practices. In his personal, professional, and creative life, Ives was almost painfully honest.[16] However, in his attempt to articulate and socialize this personal code of behavior, he became a Puritan without a cause—for it seemed impossible for him to find any modern institutions or movements to which he could apply with satisfaction the old religious zeal so very characteristic of him.

As part of a wider pattern of misplaced idealism and hope, Ives' experience with the insurance industry repeated itself in his attitude toward the First World War. "By June, 1918, Ives's identification with the war had become absolute," writes Wooldridge. "He was determined to join the Volunteer Ambulance Corps in France, had failed his first medical, and spent the first three weeks of July working on Frank Ryder's farm, to build up his physique."[17] His physical collapse on October 1, 1918, the day before his scheduled reexamination, ended any chance for participation. However, like many others, he soon became disillusioned with the war. In turn, his idealism found a new outlet in his interest in the hopes and plans of another modern Puritan, Woodrow Wilson. Wilson's own collapse, the failure of America to support the League of Nations, and the election of Harding all contributed to Ives' growing sense of isolation and detachment. Feeling like an alien in his own land, he became increasingly eccentric in both his life style and his ideas. For so many years, his failure to achieve any real recognition or understanding of his music from even his closest friends and associates added to his loneliness. Additional composition became impossible. According to Wooldridge, at one point during the summer of 1926 Ives finally broke into tears and confessed to his wife that he could no longer compose.[18] He spent the rest of his life collecting and organizing the enormous amount of work he had produced during those earlier years. He also energetically supported the efforts of younger composers who were working in the new music.

When recognition finally came dramatically to Charles Ives, he was unable to cope with it. Three years before Ives' death, the then young and brash Leonard Bernstein agreed to conduct in Carnegie Hall the first performance of the Second Symphony, the same music that helped bring so many to the Danbury centennial celebration. Composed in part before the beginning of the century, the work had gone unheard for more than fifty years. Ives refused to attend the performance and sent his wife instead.

He also rejected Bernstein's generous offer to conduct the symphony privately in the same hall. A popular legend about Ives reports that he didn't hear the highly acclaimed performance until days later, when he listened to its broadcast on his maid's radio in the kitchen of his home in Redding, Connecticut. According to the story, he seemed pleased.[19] Wooldridge, however, presents a somewhat different report of Ives' reaction to this first performance of his symphony. "Harmony Ives went down to New York with the Cowells to hear it," writes Wooldridge. "Charles Ives didn't. And he didn't listen to it on the maid's kitchen radio and do a little jig to himself afterwards either. He listened on the Ryders' radio next door, with evident and growing distress. When the last movement went on one measure longer than he'd written it, he leapt to his feet, mad, and wrenched the program off. Then went over to the fireplace and spat in it."[20]

Both the Cowells and Wooldridge fail to cite their sources for their highly divergent accounts of Ives' reaction to the broadcast. Emphasizing different perceptions of his character, these conflicting images of Ives indicate a deeper truth about the psychology of the man. Both stories celebrate opposing aspects of Ives that emerged out of his emotional and intellectual sense of identity with the history and tradition of New England. In the one story is the receptive and sensitive Ives dancing a jig of joy over the final vindication of his highly individualistic approach to music and his deep faith in the Transcendental nature of the universe. In the Wooldridge version we see the other Ives—the irascible idealist of the perverted self. This second Ives, who could not abide any imperfection in the performance of his music, also saw the world in moralistic terms that eliminated complexity or ambiguity. The two different aspects of Ives' character existed in a complex relationship. It is possible that the tension between them provided some of the impetus for both his musical creativity and his moral dedication. It is significant that the growing frustration of his moralistic sense paralleled the end of his musical composition. After 1920, he did very little additional writing. In a sense, then, Ives spent about thirty years of his life waiting for the world to come around to his way of seeing things. At least in the realm of his music, the world finally caught up with him.

Chapter 8
Beyond the Diver complex: The dynamics of modern individualism in F. Scott Fitzgerald

While we argue that the writings of Charles Ives represent a perverted form of the defense of the individual self, it should also be understood that other major figures of his time thought another alternative possible. In fact, many writers and intellectuals in the first decades of this century hoped for the emergence of a "new" individualism founded upon an understanding of the developing political and economic realities of the century. Freedom, they believed, requires more than a tyrannical assertion of the self. It also demands an intelligent and pragmatic understanding of the relationship between the self and society. Accordingly, Alan Trachtenberg argues that "a new spirit," including a new hope for the freedom of the individual, dominated these decades. "The atmosphere breathed possibility and controversy," writes Trachtenberg. "The Progressive reform movement conveyed the notion that although contemporary America had deviated from the political and social ideals of the early Republic, intelligence applied pragmatically in legislation could correct the course and restore the values of individualism against the corporations and 'bigness' in general." [1]

However, the breakthrough for such "values of individualism" for which so many hoped was impeded by the war and mired in obfuscation by the rise in the twenties of what Robert Sklar calls "the first mass culture in modern society." He writes: "Mass culture was launched in the early twenties as a consequence of the cultural crises generated in America by the First World War. Vast historical forces, to be sure, lay behind the emergence of mass culture in the twentieth century—technological growth, new media, economic development, all those shifts and great changes in the human and inanimate worlds that social scientists call by such names as industrialization, urbanization, and bureaucratization."[2] While the cultural explosion provided new opportunities, opened new forms of expression, and gave new life to millions, especially neglected and deprived ethnic and immigrant groups, the new mass culture also seriously exacerbated tensions upon the values of individualism.[3]

The literary writers of the period, of course, were deeply involved in this cultural upheaval. "A time had come when American writers could think it possible to make major works of literature out of the American experience," writes Arthur Mizener.[4] As one of the most important of this group, F. Scott Fitzgerald is especially interesting for his continued commitment in the midst of such cultural change to the idea of the integrity of the self.[5] At the same time Fitzgerald sensed the presence of threats to individualism in new cultural developments. According to Sklar, Fitzgerald shared with other intellectuals of the early twenties a concern about "how popular democracy could know enough to control increasingly complex and technical economic and political decisions."[6] Such concern for both the ideal self and popular democracy manifested itself in Fitzgerald's attempt to relate the ideas and values associated with individualism to changing cultural and political realities.[7] He knew that thinkers like Dewey in *The New Republic* were predicting "the perversion of the whole ideal of individualism" in modern mass culture.[8]

Accordingly, Fitzgerald evidences such a concern for individualism in his correspondence throughout the thirties. His self-image depended upon traditional values of individualism. In a letter written after his crack-up to Maxwell Perkins, his friend and editor at Scribner's, Fitzgerald says, "This general eclipse of ambition and determination and fortitude, all of the very qualities on which I have prided myself, is ridiculous, and, I must admit, somewhat obscene."[9] In an often quoted letter to his daughter, Frances Scott Fitzgerald, he says that "my generation of the radicals and breakers-down never found anything to take the place of the old virtues of work and courage and the old graces of courtesy and politeness."[10] Clearly, Fitzgerald never found for himself any adequate alternative values. Although for a period he considered himself something of a Marxist socialist, his ultimate rejection of communism as he understood it simply reaffirmed basic beliefs in individualism. In a letter to Perkins about Edmund Wilson's involvement with communism, he says, "A decision to adopt Communism definitely, no matter how good for the soul, must of necessity be a saddening process for anyone who has ever tasted the intellectual pleasures of the world we live in."[11] This idea that communism closes the mind and debilitates intellectual life and growth reappears seven years later in his warnings to Scottie about "the *Comrades*." He writes, "The important thing is this: they had best be treated not as people holding a certain set of liberal or conservative opinions but rather as you might treat a set of intensely fanatical Roman Catholics among whom you might find yourself. It is not that you should not disagree with them— the important thing is that you should not argue with them. The point is that Communism has become an intensely dogmatic and almost mystical religion and whatever you say they have ways of twisting it into shapes which put you in some lower category of mankind ('Fascist,' 'Liberal,' 'Trotskyist') and disparage you both intellectually and personally in the process. They are amazingly well-organized. The pith of my advice is: think what you want, the less said the better."[12] In other words, for Fitzgerald the threat resided in those who would stifle or attenuate the self and individuality. Hope remained in work and responsibility and creativity. As Andrew Turnbull says, "The individual meant everything to Fitzgerald."[13]

Thus, in *This Side of Paradise* Fitzgerald, says Sklar, "succeeded in creating a new definition of individualism in contrast to the individualism of the genteel tradition; and it led, neither to despair nor to rebellion, but to an even more responsible commitment to a social order."[14] However, in his later works, especially *Tender Is the Night* and *The Last Tycoon*, Fitzgerald even more clearly delineated the dynamics of modern individualism. The individual or fundamental self in these works can be understood and studied in terms of Jean-Paul Sartre's presentation of the Actaeon complex in *Existential Psychoanalysis*.[15] When seen in these terms Dick Diver, the hero of *Tender Is the Night*, demonstrates a form of this complex that can be called the Diver complex.

The Diver complex constitutes a particular way of perceiving and being-in-the-world, especially as an American, that enervates the creative drive of the individual self. Fitzgerald, however, went beyond this complex to present the possibility of another way of being-in-the-world, based on a modern version of a concept of a free and responsible self actively involved in rendering meaning to experience. Fitzgerald, I believe, adumbrates this form of individualism in the character of Monroe Stahr in *The Last Tycoon* as well as in some of his other writings.

As an important section of Sartre's major work, *Being and Nothingness*, *Existential Psychoanalysis* represents his attempt to develop a method of psychoanalysis consistent with his understanding of the individual and freedom. Not by any "empirical induction" but by prior definition, the individual for Sartre is his or her freedom or *"the desire to be."* [16] Through the very processes of consciousness this desire moves toward "the ideal of consciousness" that wishes "to be its own foundation" (*EP*, p. 40). "It is this ideal which can be called God," writes Sartre. "Thus the best way to conceive of the fundamental project of human reality is to say that man is the being whose project is to become God" (*EP*, p. 40). For Sartre our attitude toward making and owning relates to our desire to be God. He writes: "It is not enough that a certain picture which I have in mind should exist; it is necessary as well that it exist *through me*. Evidently in one sense the ideal would be that I should sustain the picture in being by a sort of continuous creation and that consequently it should be *mine* as though by a perpetually renewed emanation. But in another sense it must be radically distinct from myself—in order that it may be *mine* but not me" (*EP*, p. 63).[17]

In Sartre's view, "knowing" as the pursuit of knowledge follows a similar pattern as "a form of appropriation" (*EP*, p. 65). "That is why," he writes, "scientific research is nothing other than an effort to appropriate. The truth discovered, like the work of art, is *my* knowledge" (*EP*, p. 65). In this way, "the idea of discovery, or revelation," becomes a kind of rape (*EP*, pp. 66–67). "What is seen is possessed," he says, "to see is to *deflower*" (*EP*, p. 67). Thus, we arrive at Sartre's description of the Actaeon complex. He writes:

> If we examine the comparisons ordinarily used to express the relation between the knower and the known, we see that many of them are represented as being a kind of *violation by sight*. The unknown object is given as immaculate, as virgin, comparable to a *whiteness*. It has not yet "delivered up" its secret; man has not yet "snatched" its secret away from it. All these images insist that the object is ignorant of the investigations and the instruments aimed at it; it is unconscious of being known; it goes about its business without noticing the glance which spies on it, like a woman whom a passerby catches unaware at her bath. Figures of speech, sometimes vague, and sometimes more precise, like that of the "unvio-

lated depths" of nature suggest the idea of sexual intercourse more plainly. We speak of snatching away her veils from nature, of unveiling her (cf. Schiller's *Veiled Images of Saïs*). Every investigation implies the idea of a nudity which one brings out into the open by clearing away the obstacles which cover it, just as Actaeon clears away the branches so that he can have a better view of Diana at her bath. More than this, knowledge is a hunt. Bacon called it the hunt of Pan. The scientist is the hunter who surprises a white nudity and who violates by looking at it. Thus the totality of these images reveals something which we shall call the *Actaeon complex*. (*EP*, pp. 67–68)

Basically a theory of knowledge as a form of possession, the deeper meaning of the Actaeon complex involves the frustration and impossibility of possession. It relates to the way in which what is seen disappears and what is loved is lost. For Sartre the lover's dream "is to identify the beloved object with himself and still preserve for it its own individuality; let the other become me without ceasing to be the other" (*EP*, p. 70). This means that "the idea of 'carnal possession' offers us the irritating but seductive figure of a body perpetually possessed and perpetually new, on which possession leaves no trace" (*EP*, p. 69). Thus, Sartre reaffirms that knowledge and sexuality are similar in that the known is both assimilated and impenetrable. "Knowledge," he writes, "is at one and the same time a *penetration* and a *superficial* caress, a digestion and the contemplation from afar of an object which will never lose its form, the production of a thought by a continuous creation and the establishment of the total objective independence of that thought" (*EP*, pp. 70–71).

In this highly sexual theory of the Actaeon complex, we also get a study and a symbol of the way of being of Dick Diver—Doctor Dick Diver, the healer, the researcher, and the scientist who deflowers and who acts as God over the world of his creation, which is called, coincidentally, Villa Diana. Like Actaeon in the myth, Diver must possess to know. However, he also manifests this Actaeon complex in ways that are particularly relevant to the dilemma of the individual in American culture. He must justify such possession as a way of being-in-the-world in terms of his moral idealism. But, without any ideals that extend very much beyond the self, moral idealism becomes a form of personal moral absolutism. In Diver the Puritan impulse grows corrupt and intolerant; the self assumes moral superiority, while power and unity supersede pragmatism and pluralism. The process begins with the elevation of the individual but ends with a self unable to deal with either experience or reality. The self looks for greatness but ends in sickness. With all his sincere idealism, love, and desire to please, Diver still must have his own way or nothing at all. After all he is, as we have been reminded in countless studies of the novel, "a spoiled priest," according to Fitzgerald's own description of him in the famous General Plan for *Tender is the Night*.[18] The pattern for this complex seems to come more from Fitzgerald's conception and development of Diver's character and Diver's world than from any intention to follow a particular psychoanalytical school. Although Fitzgerald expressed considerable interest in the psychiatrists treating Zelda Fitzgerald throughout her breakdown, his knowledge of their work appears limited. It seems, instead, that Fitzgerald forged the novel and its characters out of the interplay between his own artistic imagination and his lived experience.[19]

Moreover, the Diver version of the Actaeon complex focuses the basic pattern of relationships around a moral and psychological dilemma of personal concern to Fitzgerald as a father and of special relevance to the American political experience. How do you demonstrate authentic concern for people without controlling and ruining them with the very intensity of your involvement especially when faced with a world in which no one seems to care or love? This question pervades American democratic culture. In a popular democracy of free individuals each person theoretically must create her or his own balance, identity, and set of meaningful relationships. Although many seem to avoid the crisis and the moment of truth, the responsibility remains. In American culture the tension can become excruciating. As Paul Tillich indicates, alienation becomes a form of sin while, as Trilling suggests, authenticity becomes a dissimulation of salvation. Meanwhile, the culture remains obdurate in its insistence that the individual be both involved and authentic at the same time. The Diver complex signals a breakdown in the commitment to the continuing attempt to deal with all these demands not only of the self and culture, of the individual and the community, but of the mutability of experience and life. The complex is the special tragedy of the democratic individual who turns Puritan, who becomes in Sartre's terms a kind of God, who drains the self of emotional intensity in the effort to save all the world, whose heart grows cold to the very sinners to be saved because the self has been lost in the abstraction of righteousness and moral vision so that the individual can no longer contend with the humanity of others and the existential challenge of individual being.

In seeing reality in terms of what Hegel called the law of the heart—that is, his personal sense of moral truth—Diver becomes a moral tyrant without a country. He perpetuates a pattern that Nathaniel Hawthorne described as the "Unpardonable Sin" of those Puritans who lost touch with basic human reality and emotion. In Hawthorne's story "Ethan Brand," Brand recalls "with what tenderness, with what love and sympathy for mankind, and what pity for human guilt and woe, he had first begun to contemplate those ideas which afterwards became the inspiration of his life; with what reverence he had then looked into the heart of man, viewing it as a temple originally divine, and, however, desecrated, still to be held sacred by a brother; with what awful fear he had deprecated the success of his pursuit, and prayed that the Unpardonable Sin might never be revealed to him."[20] Soon, however, Brand's "intellectual development" serves to harden his heart and disturbs "the counterpoise between his mind and heart." His love grows corrupt and turns into its very enemy—hatred and intolerance. The heart "ceased to partake of the universal throb." Hawthorne writes: "He was no longer a brother-man, opening the chambers or the dungeons of our common nature by the key of holy sympathy, which gave him a right to share in all its secrets; he was now a cold observer, looking on mankind as the subject of his experiment, and, at length, converting man and woman to be his puppets, and pulling the wires that moved them to such degrees of crime as were demanded for his study."[21]

Although Diver, of course, never abuses his powers of intellect to this extent, early in the novel Fitzgerald indicates such a propensity in him. In this scene Fitzgerald also uses the image of a key as a metaphor for secret power over others. Significantly, the metaphor concerns the relationship between Diver and Nicole Warren, whose love for him increases the power Diver as a doctor can hold over her. "He himself was the incalculable element involved. By no conscious volition of his own, the thing had drifted into his hands. It reminded him of a scene in his childhood when everyone in the house was looking for the lost key to the silver closet, Dick knowing he had hid it under the handkerchiefs in his mother's top drawer; at that time he had experienced a philosophical detachment, and this was repeated now."²² Thus, early in the revised version of the novel we see the way Diver, in spite of his great idealism, can use his power, both emotional and intellectual, over people.

This impulse toward power receives reenforcement from Diver's sense of himself as a hero with a destiny that makes him an actor on the stage of history—an idea sustained by Rosemary Hoyt's image of him as an actor. Accordingly, Nicole's sickness creates his opportunity to play a hero's role which he cannot resist. Earlier in the novel we learned that Diver thinks of himself in heroic terms as "lucky Dick," who is somehow blessed to sustain the "heroic period" during which he developed his most important work (p. 4). Although his plans include becoming not only "a good psychiatrist" but perhaps "the greatest one that ever lived," he clearly has a sense of himself that goes beyond this professional goal (p. 22). In this moment of Diver's life, Fitzgerald compares him to Grant at Galena. He tells us that "the hero like Grant, lolling in his general store in Galena, is ready to be called to an intricate destiny. Best to be reassuring—Dick Diver's moment now began" (p. 6). A little further into the novel, Fitzgerald gives us another picture of Diver's vision of himself as a hero with a special destiny that makes him superior in many ways. Fitzgerald writes, "In the dead white hours in Zurich staring into a stranger's pantry across the upshine of a street-lamp, he used to think that he wanted to be good, he wanted to be kind, he wanted to be brave and wise, but it was all pretty difficult. He wanted to be loved, too, if he could fit it in" (p. 23). In the same scene Diver appeals to heaven with the question, "God am I like the rest after all?" This is more than youthful inexperience, exuberance, and ambition speaking. As if to make precisely this point, Fitzgerald writes that "he used to think starting awake at night—'Am I like the rest?'" (p. 23).

Diver's sense of mission and destiny relates him to another Hawthorne character, Young Goodman Brown, who also remains awake at night to consider a special destiny for himself. Both Diver and Brown are in situations of moral isolation.²³ Moreover, Diver's experience in the moral wasteland of the novel is not unlike Brown's journey into the wilderness. *Tender is the Night* does represent a kind of modern witches' sabbath.²⁴ Both men can be seen as venturing on classic journeys of initiation during which they will undergo severe trials of their intellect, morality, and basic humanity. Both, I think, fail. They fail to survive their journeys intact or to grow significantly as human beings. The experiences of initiation should give them the strength and maturity to assume real moral leadership. Instead, they are each isolated and debilitated by their experiences and are unable to function as complete individuals capable of integrating within themselves the knowledge gained from their experiences. In effect, they emotionally and spiritually leave the human community because they are unable to live with the moral freedom and ambiguity of human experience. Thus, while the repeated refrain, "Do you mind if I pull down the curtain?" (pp. 150–162), to some extent indicates the pertinacity of Diver's gentility, it also demonstrates his proclivity to isolate himself from the vicissitudes of common experience and to hide from the implications of his own behavior, failure, and attitudes.

For Brown and Diver this pattern of estrangement has its most pathetic effect upon their attitudes toward their wives. In the stories of Diver and Brown the women represent the moral condition of their societies. Also, both men realize their destinies through these women. Significantly, the men believe their wives fail them in one form or another, but any falls from grace can be attributed in large part to the actions of the husbands. For example, Brown insists on making the journey through the forest in spite of Faith's caveats. Diver also makes choices that inexorably lead to his separation from Nicole. As prophets of doom lacking faith in human possiblity, both men become oddities alienated from their own people. Hawthorne writes of Brown: "A stern, a sad, a darkly meditative, a distrustful, if not a desperate man did he become from the night of that fearful dream. . . . Often, waking suddenly at midnight, he shrank from the bosom of Faith; and at morning or eventide, when the family knelt down at prayer, he scowled and muttered to himself, and gazed sternly at his wife, and turned away." [25] Similarly, Dick starts to see himself in terms of evil and misery and death. "I guess I'm the Black Death," he says. "I don't seem to bring people happiness any more" (p. 237). A few pages later, in the midst of his drunken spree, he is alone and wishes to "lie down with his black heart" (p. 242).

Thus, Nicole comes to see Diver as a "mad puritan" (p. 312). Moreover, in seeing him this way, she chooses "a sane crook," meaning Tommy Barban, the barbarian-adventurer. Diver relinquishes the field of battle to this man in an act of self-defeat. Diver, who would be God and who would pursue an ideal sense of himself as both a hero and a savior, ultimately fails as a Puritan. By becoming a "mad puritan" with a black heart who alienates himself from others, he really betrays the ideals he wants to protect and perpetuate. In an earlier scene Fitzgerald writes: "Dick didn't want to talk—he wanted to be alone so that his thoughts about work and the future would overpower his thoughts of love and today" (p. 182). In a sense, the remainder of the novel demonstrates Diver's inability to be alone to work. One of the harshest judgments against him comes from the wife of a colleague. "Dick is no longer a serious man," she says (p. 259). The comment is equal to the judgment made earlier by Doctor Dohmler that Devereux Warren was a "peasant!" (p. 19). Both comments suggest failures of character and a betrayal of values that render one less than civilized.

Dick Diver, who once almost casually dismissed the danger of becoming "one of the young doctors that could be purchased in the intellectual stockyards of the South Side of Chicago," discovers that he has sold himself (p. 47). He surrendered what could not be captured or bought by another. In hoping to be everything, he became nothing: "He had lost himself—he could not tell the hour when, or the day or the week, the month or the year. Once he had cut through things, solving the most complicated equations as the simplest problems of his simplest patients. Between the time he found Nicole flowering under a stone on the Zurichsee and the moment of his meeting with Rosemary the spear had been blunted" (p. 218). The conflict between his intense concern for people and his disappointment in their failure to fulfill his expectations helps him lose himself. He is caught between feeling intense care and utter contempt. On the one hand, Fitzgerald writes that "he felt so intensely about people that in moments of apathy he preferred to remain concealed" and that "he cared only about people; he was scarcely conscious of places except for their weather, until they had been invested with color by tangible events" (pp. 149, 239). On the other hand, Diver comes increasingly to find people contemptible. He wavers not only in his compassion but in his ability to sense their reality. Silently approaching Diver's "sanctuary," Nicole observes him: "He was thinking, he was living a world completely his own" (p. 318). He so profoundly feels his own failure and the failure of people toward him and toward themselves that he grows unable to tolerate their reality and presence. "Don't touch me!" he barks at Nicole (p. 319). The words evoke the feeling of his own righteousness and sanctity and his fear of contamination by humanity. To his credit, the words also signify a remnant of continuing pride, for Nicole's gesture was made out of pity born of her sudden realization of Diver's losses: "She felt as sorry for him as she had sometimes felt for Abe North and his ignoble destiny, sorry as for the helplessness of infants and the old" (p. 319).

At another point Nicole actually thinks in terms of sinning against Diver. Against his explicit wishes, she gives a rare camphor rub to Barban. "It's American—Dick believes in it," she says (p. 296). Diver pouts over the insult and Nicole returns cautiously to him: "Upstairs again she looked into his room—the blue eyes, like searchlights, played on a dark sky. She stood a minute in the doorway, aware of the sin she had committed against him, afraid to come in" (p. 297). Diver's estrangement grows so profound and his isolation so deep that he simply admits to people that he can no longer stand them. He is told by Mary North Minghetti, an old friend he now despises, that "everybody loved you. You could've had anybody you wanted for the asking" (p. 332). The statement, however, fails to affect his earlier feeling: "You're all so dull." The answer entails his dilemma: "But we're all there is!" (p. 332). She continues: "All people want is to have a good time and if you make them unhappy you cut yourself off from nourishment." For Diver to acknowledge a need for such nourishment would admit not only dependence upon other people but a common humanity and a common weakness. Instead, he must feel himself to be their God.

Thus, Diver's good-bye takes the form of blessing the beach. In an age of ruthless leaders and tyrants, his gesture suggests a political as well as a religious action. "He raised his right hand and with a papal cross, he blessed the beach from the high terrace. Faces turned upward from several umbrellas." Seeing the gesture, Nicole rises. "I'm going to him," she says. Tommy physically restrains her. "Let well enough alone" (p. 333).

Unable to be both king and pope, Diver literally leaves the best part of himself behind in a world he had built like the original Puritans but for which he no longer accepts any responsibility. Believing Nicole cured he thinks, "The case was finished. Doctor Diver was at liberty" (p. 320). Of course, the cost of that liberty constitutes the loss of himself. He actually seems to disappear in upstate New York, a phantom and a rumor of his former power and lost self. In Sartrian terms this constitutes a false form of liberty. Diver loses himself by failing to create himself in freedom.

He commits the deterministic fallacy of projecting his own weaknesses upon his environment, his background, and his friends. In *Existential Psychoanalysis* Sartre insists, "The environment can act on the subject only to the exact extent that he comprehends it; that is, transforms it into a situation. Hence no objective description of this environment could be of any use to us. From the start the environment as a situation refers to the for-itself which is choosing, just as the for-itself refers to the environment by the very fact that it is in the world" (*EP*, p. 54).[26]

Although Sartre's growing interest in Marxism after the war has induced him to modify his views, he continues to maintain one's responsibility for one's condition.[27] It is just this responsibility, however, that Diver fails to exercise. He runs from his freedom. Thus, his histrionics with Rosemary at the Thiepval battlefield represent a form of self-burial through self-pity and fear. "'All my beautiful lovely safe world blew itself up here with a great gust of high explosive love,' he mourned persistently. 'Isn't that true, Rosemary?'" (p. 118). A similar attitude demonstrates itself later at the death of his father. "Next day at the churchyard his father was laid among a hundred Divers, Dorseys, and Hunters. It was very friendly leaving him there with all his relations around him. Flowers were scattered on the brown unsettled earth. Dick had no more ties here now and did not believe he would come back. He knelt on the hard soil. These dead, he knew them all, their weather-beaten faces with blue flashing eyes, the spare violent bodies, the souls made of new earth in the forest-heavy darkness of the seventeenth century. 'Good-bye, my father—good-bye, all my fathers'" (p. 222). This worship of the dead and of the past represents another facet of the Diver complex in the form of the flight from present experience and time that enables Dick Diver to lose himself.

Some of the most interesting and impressive criticism of Fitzgerald and *Tender Is the Night* comes from those who see themselves as defenders both of Diver's moral position in the novel and of the values he seems to represent in the culture as a whole. Thus, in his powerful and highly moralistic study of Fitzgerald, Milton Stern refers to a line in which Nicole recalls "what she owed Dick" (p. 311). Stern goes on to comment: "She doesn't owe much, after all. Only her life and sanity. Only all the self-sacrifice of controlled and controlling love that took Nicole after she had been destroyed by sexual release, impulsive gratification, after she had been victimized by the irresponsible moral shabbiness of the Buchanan world (the name is now spelled Warren) that is the heritage of her fathers and is seen in 'white crook's eyes.'"[28] Clearly, the tone indicates Stern's conviction that others besides Diver suffer abuse in the modern age. Imputations of fascism and barbarism extend beyond the domain of Barban and the Warrens and encompass the student activists, feminists, and radicals of the sixties.[29]

While he symbolizes for Stern a last stronghold for traditional values and discipline, Diver to me stands for the contemporary myth of salvation through false authenticity. As the God who failed, Diver refuses to compromise with a social reality or communicate with people—they're so dull—who exist beneath his contempt. Thus, the madwoman at his clinic symbolizes not the madness of Nicole but Diver's own moral and psychological isolation. This woman has become his "most interesting case." Like Zelda Fitzgerald, she had been "exceptionally pretty" but now suffers from a horrible form of eczema that turns her into "a living, agonizing sore" (p. 199). "She was particularly his patient. During spells of over-excitement he was the only doctor who could 'do anything with her'" (p. 199). She pathetically says to him: "I am here as a symbol of something. I thought perhaps you would know what it was" (p. 201). "You are sick," Diver responds. As a symbol of the sickness they share, she found an even "greater sickness." Diver's diagnosis, which he kindly keeps to himself, could also fit his own mental situation. He thinks the woman suffers from her attempt to explore "the frontiers of consciousness." He could be speaking of himself when he thinks: "The frontiers that artists must explore were not for her, ever. She was fine-spun, inbred—eventually she might find rest in some quiet mysticism. Exploration was for those with a measure of peasant blood, those with big thighs and thick ankles who could take punishment as they took bread and salt, on every inch of flesh and spirit. —Not for you, he almost said. It's too tough a game for you." Too tough a game for Diver as well, it remains the only one he will play. While this woman cries, Fitzgerald's sentence indicates that Diver cries as well: "As he arose the tears fled lava-like into her bandages."[30] The heavy emotion of the scene indicates the continuation of the same pattern concerning Diver's way of relating to people, especially women, in paternalistic terms that combine domination, sexuality, and love. "Yet in the awful majesty of her pain," writes Fitzgerald, "he went out to her unreservedly, almost sexually. He wanted to gather her up in his arms, as he so often had Nicole, and cherish even her mistakes, so deeply were they part of her" (p. 201).

However, as these emotions rise and flood in Diver, Fitzgerald emphasizes hearing "the voice searching the vacuity of her illness and finding only remote abstractions" (p. 201). Both Diver and this woman are suffering from an illness of abstraction that removes them from reality. Leaving her side, Diver visits more patients, concluding his morning with "a collapsed psychiatrist" whose mental breakdown represents Diver's own precarious mental state (p. 202). Like his female patient, Diver has made the trip to the frontiers of consciousness and experiences its price in terms of his own mental stability and his ability to deal with reality on a continuing basis. For him the heroic nature of the journey toward personal liberation struggles against its meaning as a flight from responsibility and from freedom. The aspect of his character that enables him to simply walk away from his continuing responsibilities—to leave the battle that becomes too boring and mundane and painful—can escape the consideration of those critics who so passionately argue his case because of their sense of commitment to the high values they think Diver represents.

A major theme in the literature and thought that has followed Fitzgerald concerns the idea of exhaustion—the end of possibilities both for the individual and for humanistic studies of the individual.[31] For the exponents of this idea, exhaustion usually comes to mean a way of creating new literature out of old forms through such devices as parody. But the idea also relates to a discernible general malaise concerning culture as a whole. Significantly, in both a professional and a personal sense, Fitzgerald found the strength to defy exhaustion even in the face of his own collapse. As he says in *The Crack-Up*, during this period of "the disintegration of one's own personality" he learned that "in a real dark night of the soul it is always three o'clock in the morning, day after day."[32] He also learned, however, to overcome this crisis through continued creativity and production. "The test of a first-rate intelligence is the ability to hold two opposed ideas in the mind at the same time, and still retain the ability to function," he writes.[33] He went on to pass that test and fulfill himself in his own terms. "I must hold in balance," he says in *The Crack-Up*, "the sense of the futility of effort and the sense of the necessity to struggle; the conviction of the inevitability of failure and still the determination to 'succeed'—and, more than these, the contradictions between the dead hand of the past and the high intentions of the future. If I could do this through the common ills—domestic, professional and personal—then the ego would continue as an arrow shot from nothingness to nothingness with such force that only gravity would bring it to earth at last."[34] A major form of his success appeared in his unfinished novel about Hollywood, *The Last Tycoon*. Edmund Wilson, friend, critic, and aid in the posthumous publication of the work, considers both the novel and its hero, Monroe Stahr, mature achievements for Fitzgerald. According to Wilson, "*The Last Tycoon* is thus, even in its imperfect state, Fitzgerald's most mature piece of work."[35] As such the novel represents a special triumph for Fitzgerald as both artist and man.

However, there also exists in the character of Stahr important extra literary meanings. As the symbolism of their names suggests, the move from Diver to Stahr entails an attempt to concentrate on one's struggle to influence the course of institutions and history and the direction of one's life. This shifts the focus from the environment and psychology in *Tender Is the Night* to the creative power of the individual in *The Last Tycoon*. Stahr represents, as Mizener says, "the image of genuine authority in a democratic society."[36] In Stahr, Fitzgerald created a character relevant to contemporary culture who possesses the potential for moving toward a meaningful individualism. Stahr presents an alternative to the idea of cultural and individual exhaustion. As a character he deals with exhaustion in its own terms through a defense of the inherent value of work. Knowing that Stahr will die soon, his doctor wants him to "lie down and look at the sky for six months" in order to enjoy his last days. He only vaguely understands that for Stahr this would involve a premature burial. For Stahr the lightheaded feeling associated with weariness means life in the sense of work, purpose, and creation. Doctor Baer thinks: "You couldn't persuade a man like Stahr to stop and lie down and look at the sky for six months. He would much rather die. He said differently, but what it added up to was the definite urge toward total exhaustion that he had run into before. Fatigue was a drug as well as a poison, and Stahr apparently derived some rare almost physical pleasure from working lightheaded with weariness. It was a perversion of the life force he had seen before, but he had almost stopped trying to interfere with it. He had cured a man or so— a hollow triumph of killing and preserving the shell."[37]

Rather than a "perversion," Stahr sees this attitude toward work as a natural and meaningful way of dealing with the world. Work changes the world. The belief in work as a means for a salvation that goes beyond the physical provides the basis for Stahr as a symbol of the autonomous individualist in a world of growing corporate conformity. Through work he turns the dehumanizing aspects of popular culture into a new opportunity for a renaissance of at least his own individual strengths and talents. "I'm the unity," he says about his way of putting together stories by several different writers. He describes himself as a "production man"—a term, of course, that again describes traditional individualism. But his genius at production manifests itself in his powers as "a sort of technological virtuoso."[38] His old-fashioned brand of individuality becomes something new through his mastery of the technology that enables him to lead the very consumer culture that threatens such individualism. Thus, as Michael Wood says, one version of the Hollywood producer "as dynamic, all-purpose genius, like Fitzgerald's Monroe Stahr, modeled on Irving Thalberg," emerges from *The Last Tycoon*.[39] We also need to emphasize that Stahr has qualities of moral consciousness and artistic sensitivity that distinguish him dramatically from the kind of media manipulators of public opinion who came to characterize, at least for many liberals, the values and mentality of the operatives who dominate the modern communications industry. This latter type threatens Stahr. As a creative consciousness in a new technological environment, he represents a new face and version in an inchoate form of the symbolic Emersonian American self.

Moreover, Stahr as a person proves the very potential for growth within the culture itself. A Jew who comes from the masses, Stahr embodies the common man. He is a mass man who rises as a free individual. Because of his background he operates from a broad basis of common humanity and shared experience that Diver, with his own poor but genteel origins, often felt only abstractly. Like Whitman's ideal for the democratic man and woman, he is every man and his own man whose experience in the slums and streets strengthened his character. Moreover, if we think of the anti-Semite in Sartrian terms as someone who feels fear "not of the Jews, to be sure, but of himself, of his own consciousness, of his liberty, of his instincts, of his responsibilities," and ultimately "of the human condition," then the challenge to such tendencies through a character like Stahr indicates a significant broadening and maturity of Fitzgerald's own early social and political vision.[40]

In this sense, Stahr stands in even greater contrast to Diver, whose submerged racism erupts repeatedly in the novel. Diver's references to "some nigger scrap" and to a "spic" concern two unrelated incidents during which feelings of pain, tension, and despair act to extrude this racism (pp. 172, 236). The attitude itself suggests even deeper fear and hatred in Diver's way of relating to the world.

Fitzgerald, in his own notes for *The Last Tycoon*, indicates that he saw extinction in Stahr's future because there would be "no place for real individualists of business like Stahr whose successes are personal achievements and whose career has always been invested with a certain personal glamor." Fitzgerald continues: "He has held himself directly responsible to everyone with whom he has worked; he has even wanted to beat up his enemies himself. In Hollywood he is 'the last tycoon.'"[41] Many of the critics follow the author's lead on this matter.[42] Of course, the figure of the last tycoon has become something of a cliché in the popular arts, a fact which perhaps signifies both continuing interest in and continuing danger to the "values of individualism" in American culture.

However, as in the case of Mark Twain, reports of Stahr's demise are perhaps greatly exaggerated. In *The Last Tycoon*, Stahr's anticipated defeat before great forces becomes less significant than the manner in which he engages those forces during his life. Such engagement suggests a commitment on Fitzgerald's part to a permanent process of interaction between the self and the environment rather than the elevation of a romantic Gatsby-like ideal of a glorious failure. Through Stahr's character and story, Fitzgerald seems to make a moral statement that reaffirms the idea of our responsibility for our own destiny. In effect, we move from the Diver complex to a form of democratic individualism. As such it revivifies a philosophy of individual responsibility that William James promulgated in terms of pragmatism and humanism.[43]

Thus, in contrast to Stahr's humanistic and pragmatic understanding of experience, Diver becomes a victim of the rigid and absolutist tendencies to which he adheres for protection from experience. After "Baby" Warren rescues him from his difficulties with the police she thinks, "It had been a hard night but she had the satisfaction of feeling that whatever Dick's previous record was, they now possessed a moral superiority over him for as long as he proved of any use" (p. 253). As long as morals are measured on this kind of scale, "Baby" Warren's thinking cannot be faulted.

In addition, Diver's manner of abstracting himself from the world because of his despair about himself and contempt for others enables him to avoid the pain of feeling involved in some basic moral questions, including those surrounding the meaning of Nicole's return to the world. Essentially, as Nicole's doctor, he prescribes an idea of health as accommodation to a cruel and ugly world for which Nicole and her family readily assume considerable responsibility.

> Nicole was the product of much ingenuity and toil. For her sake trains began their run at Chicago and traversed the round belly of the continent to California; chicle factories fumed and link belts grew link by link in factories; men mixed toothpaste in vats and drew mouthwash out of copper hogsheads; girls canned tomatoes quickly in August or worked rudely at the Five-and-Tens on Christmas Eve; half-breed Indians toiled on Brazilian coffee plantations and dreamers were muscled out of patent rights in new tractors—these were some of the people who gave a tithe to Nicole and, as the whole system swayed and thundered onward, it lent a feverish bloom to such processes of hers as wholesale buying, like the flush of a fireman's face holding his post before a spreading blaze. She illustrated very simple principles, containing in herself her own doom, but illustrated them so accurately that there was grace in the procedure, and presently Rosemary would try to imitate it. (pp. 113–114)

In these lines Fitzgerald develops an exciting catalog of images and ideas to build tension. He condenses an economic system into one image of "wholesale buying," dramatizes and personifies an interpretation of that system through the image of the fireman, and heightens awareness of that system's insidious power by inculpating an apparently innocent consciousness through the allusion to Rosemary's receptivity and her incipient approval.

The above lines also raise questions about Diver's role as a doctor who teaches Nicole to accept herself and her role in this worldwide dynasty. He repairs her so that she can assume her position in the family exactly as her sister intended. He surrenders her to Barban, thereby allowing, perhaps even encouraging, the unification on the symbolic level at least of ungovernable forces of violence and power. The union takes us over the "threshold of the future." Earlier in the novel Diver and Rosemary had crossed that threshold with a brief visit to a strange house of mirrors and images in which people become exploited and fragmented selves (pp. 133–137). A world of accelerated change, it creates a completely fluid individual self unable to understand or assume responsibility and freedom. Significantly, Stahr's world of images and false identities in films compares to this house of mirrors. But Stahr serves as a consciousness for this world, giving it order, unity, and coherence in a way that involves it in, but distinguishes it from, life. The house of mirrors is a happening that has become life. In that sense, it becomes a vatic portrait of what Ihab Hassan, Irving Howe, George Steiner, Hayden White, and others see as our contemporary culture warring on itself. Through his isolation Dick Diver acts almost as a midwife for the passage of Nicole and Tommy into this world. As such he takes what William James would call "a moral holiday," in which he no longer examines or accepts responsibility for the truths by which he lives.[44]

In *The Crack-Up* Fitzgerald described a "philosophy fitted" to his "early adult life" that represents a simplistic, popularized version of a pragmatic attitude toward the individual. Veritable miracles, of course, had occurred in Fitzgerald's own career. Seeing "the improbable, the implausible, often the 'impossible' come true," he believed that "life was something you dominated if you were any good. Life yielded easily to intelligence and effort, or to what proportion could be mustered of both."[45] Obviously, such a philosophy represents a form of false elitism predicated on the egoism of youth. It resembles the illusions that were Diver's "Achilles' heels"—"illusions of eternal strength and health, and of the essential goodness of people—they were the illusions of a nation, the lies of generations of frontier mothers who had to croon falsely that there were no wolves outside the cabin door" (p. 5). However, Fitzgerald soon learned that the situation was more complicated. The emoluments of success could lose their grandeur upon possession or could become something with unforeseen predicaments. Worst of all, the magic could turn sour, and one could discover that the lack of a foundation in character and the self, what Thoreau described as the "gold within," could render experience without value or meaning.

Thus, faced with failure, Fitzgerald's earlier egotism turned into self-pity. For a while he came to see himself as a victim. In *The Crack-Up* he compared his situation to that of "the American Negro" forced "to endure the intolerable conditions of his existence" with a "laughing stoicism" that cost the black man "his sense of the truth" and caused Fitzgerald to discard "the old dream of being an entire man."[46] Although Fitzgerald argued that the attempt to execute a clean break or even an escape could become its own trap, he goes on to describe exactly such a scheme, at least in psychological and existential terms. He writes: "So, since I could no longer fulfill the obligations that life had set for me or that I had set for myself, why not slay the empty shell who had been posturing at it for four years."[47] He clearly thinks in terms of escaping one's self or identity in order to create what R. D. Laing calls a false self. By executing a clean break or an escape from the real but unappreciated self that has failed in its search for love, the counterfeit self with an artificial smile and voice would survive. "I must continue to be a writer," he says, "because that was my only way of life, but I would cease any attempts to be a person—to be kind, just or generous. There were plenty of counterfeit coins around that would pass instead of these and I knew where I could get them at a nickel on the dollar."[48] He goes on to describe his plans to "get me a smile" that panders to people's prejudices and to train his voice to "show no ring of conviction except the conviction of the person I am talking to."[49]

However, because of his great commitment to work and achievement, Fitzgerald eventually moved beyond such self-pity and contempt to a new sense of himself. In a famous letter written to his daughter, he says, "What little I've accomplished has been by the most laborious and uphill work, and I wish now I'd *never* relaxed or looked back—but said at the end of *The Great Gatsby*: 'I've found my line—from now on this comes first. This is my immediate duty—without this I am nothing.'"[50] In another letter written several months later but only two months before his death, Fitzgerald indicated an even stronger commitment to action based on a new faith in one's self: "By this I mean the thing that lies behind all great careers, from Shakespeare's to Abraham Lincoln's, and as far back as there are books to read—the sense that life is essentially a cheat and its conditions are those of defeat, and that the redeeming things are not 'happiness and pleasure' but the deeper satisfactions that come out of struggle. Having learned this in theory from the lives and conclusions of great men, you can get a hell of a lot more enjoyment out of whatever right things come your way."[51]

Fortunately, Fitzgerald did not settle, like Diver, for a flight into a false and meaningless liberty. He learned instead to find a true value in himself through his own work and effort. Accordingly, in an undated letter he made a comment about himself that is relevant to the best in American culture both in his time and in our own. "I never blame failure—there are too many complicated situations in life," he writes, "but I am absolutely merciless toward lack of effort."[52]

᪥ Chapter 9

*The radical individualism
of William James: A theory of
experience and the self
for today*

The work of William James plays a crucial role in the history of American individualism, especially during the past century. On this subject Frederick J. Hoffman writes, "I think the major turning point in this history is William James's superbly detailed, yet suspiciously naive, analysis of consciousness in his *Principles of Psychology* (1890). Searching for a definition of 'self,' James there had to conclude that the self is not substantively tenable but is only a *process* of experiencing. He therefore anticipated, in his own special, indigenously well-intentioned American way, the melodrama of Jean-Paul Sartre's description of choice, freedom and responsibility." [1] However, rather than exploring this anticipation of Sartre and existentialism, Hoffman argues that James dealt with this dilemma of a nonsubstantial self in the manner of an "antecedent of the twentieth-century romantic" who becomes forced by his refusal to surrender the idea of the self to rely upon "Victorian reassurances" of its existence and also upon "a Victorian-democratic definition of the will." [2] With his disdain for the modernist understanding of the self, Hoffman naturally reads James' ideas as something of a disaster that furthered the existential idea of the self and influenced "the imagistic-oriented literature of the 1920s." [3] For Hoffman James' attempt to see "the ultimate character of reality" as a "willed thing" amounts to an argument for the self in terms of transcendence. [4]

Another scholar and critic, Quentin Anderson, sees James as furthering a tradition of the self whose "wide authority over reality" in American culture and literature "has a religious origin."

Anderson argues that this religious impulse toward the self resulted in the deification of such "visionary" thinkers as Emerson,
Thoreau, and Whitman to the denigration of more "practical"
thinkers.[5] Believing that for such visionaries "action in the world
is a threat to our sense of ourselves," Anderson goes on to include
both John Dewey and James as "examples of this visionary distortion of the national scene."[6] Thus, to Hoffman and Anderson the
concept of self in James epitomizes the crisis of individualism and
freedom in the modern age. For them James' relevance is deroga-
tory because of their understanding of his work as the continued
presentation of an isolated and diminished self. For them the
themes of modernism as used by James inherently insist on the
ultimate impoverishment of the self.

However, what Hoffman and Anderson see as negative aspects
of James' philosophy of experience and the self, others interpret as
a major breakthrough in the attempt of contemporary thought to
develop a theory of democratic individualism both relevant to
modern consciousness and "radical" in its faith in the capacity
of the individual to deal with modern experience. To such ad-
vocates, James' work represents one of the clearest statements
of individual freedom of the modern period. Thus James, to the
philosopher William Barrett, "belongs to our time, he is our contemporary in the 20th century." "He speaks," Barrett continues,
"to us now, I believe, more forcefully than at any time since his
death in 1910."[7] For diverse others as well—Gay Wilson Allen,
his biographer; John Wild, the philosopher; Rollo May, the existential psychologist—this sense of his presence is derived to a considerable extent from the originality of his direct confrontation
with the very issues, themes, and language of modernism, including his refusal to rule out the possibility in "the modern tradition"
of freedom and individualism.[8]

What I consider to be James' commitment to radical individualism is derived from his understanding of the empirical and individual nature of human experience. In James the basis for individuality rests, as Hoffman says, upon the process involved in the
individual's way of experiencing reality in the world. James was
pragmatic when it came to naming this process. He varied between calling his philosophy a wider pragmatism, radical empiricism, radical pluralism, and humanism. Each term places a different emphasis on a particular aspect of James' understanding of the
process involved in the individual's relationship to experience and
reality. But each term in its own way also emphasizes the individ-

ual and the concrete in experience as opposed to the abstract and the "viciously intellectual." Noting in "Monistic Idealism" that "neither abstract oneness nor abstract independence *exists*, only concrete real things exist," James contrasts his philosophy with that of rationalistic systems that attempt to find truths based on abstractions.[9] In another essay, "A World of Pure Experience," he writes: "I give the name of 'radical empiricism' to my Weltanschauung. Empiricism is known as the opposite of rationalism. Rationalism tends to emphasize universals and to make wholes prior to parts in the order of logic as well as in that of being. Empiricism, on the contrary, lays the explanatory stress upon the part, the element, the individual, and treats the whole as a collection and the universal as an abstraction." He goes on to describe the "epithet radical" as a term that forces the commitment to the real, the concrete, and the individual. "To be radical, an empiricism must neither admit into its constructions any element that is not directly experienced, nor exclude from them any element that is directly experienced," he writes (*ERE*, pp. 24–25).

With its concentration on real, radical, and pure experience, James' radical empiricism moves toward an open, pluralistic philosophy of the universe that makes individuals self-supporting but condemns them to insecurity and freedom within a continuing creative flux of change and experience. In "Humanism and Truth" James says, "Must not something end by supporting itself? Humanism is willing to let finite experience be self-supporting."[10] He realized, of course, that such a view runs counter not only to the desire of many for permanence but to important systems of philosophy as well. In his brilliant essay on Hegel's method, James notes that Hegel "considers that the immediate finite data of experience are 'untrue' because they are not their own others. They are negated by what is external to them. The absolute is true because it and it only has no external environment, and has attained to being its own other" (*PU*, p. 173). James goes on to state that, if one grants Hegel's argument that "to be true a thing must in some sort be its own other, everything hinges on whether he is right in holding that the several pieces of finite experience themselves cannot be said to be in any wise *their* own others." Following Hegel's intellectualist method, James could never prove the truth of self-dependent "pieces" of "the immediate finite data of experience." He says: "When conceptually or intellectualistically treated, they of course cannot be their own others. Every abstract concept as such excludes what it doesn't include, and if such concepts are adequate substitutes for reality's concrete pulses, the latter must square themselves with intellectualistic logic, and no one of them in any sense can claim to be its own other" (*PU*, pp. 173–174).

In his subsequent essay on Henri Bergson, however, James makes this argument about the possibility for experience to be its "own other" by changing the terms of the discussion so that the stream of experience is proffered over abstractions as a means for discovering truth. Using Bergson's work, James impugns traditional logic and conceptualization as ultimate forms of truth. "The whole process of life is due to life's violation of our logical axioms," he writes (*PU*, p. 245). He maintains that the "faculty of abstracting and fixing concepts" is a process of convenience that gives us only one kind of practical truth. "What we do in fact is to *harness up* reality in our conceptual systems in order to drive it the better," he says (*PU*, p. 238). Stating that "when we conceptualize, we cut out and fix, and exclude everything but what we have fixed," he argues that in the flow of "the real concrete sensible flux of life experiences compenetrate each other so that it is not easy to know just what is excluded and what not" (*PU*, pp. 243, 244). In this flux of "direct" or "immediate" or "sensible" experience, it becomes perfectly possible then for aspects of experience to be self-supporting or, in Hegel's terms, its "own other." James writes:

> The absolute is said to perform its feats by taking up its other into itself. But that is exactly what is done when every individual morsel of the sensational stream takes up the adjacent morsels by coalescing with them. This is just what we mean by the stream's sensible continuity. No element *there* cuts itself off from any other element, as concepts cut themselves from concepts. No part *there* is so small as not to be a place of conflux. No part there is not really *next* its neighbors; which means that there is literally nothing between; which means again that no part goes exactly so far and no farther; that no part absolutely excludes another, but that they compenetrate and are cohesive; that if you tear out one, its roots bring out more with them; that whatever is real is telescoped and diffused into other reals; that, in short, every minutest thing is already its hegelian 'own other,' in the fullest sense of the term. (*PU*, p. 252)

James' description of experience as self-sustaining within a continuous stream of experience has important implications for the idea of radical individualism. This view of experience places the individual in the middle of the action. It enables the individual to develop a creative relationship with reality through the use of what James terms the "living understanding" of the process of continuous creation within experience. "Philosophy," he says, "should seek this kind of living understanding of the movement of reality, not follow science in vainly patching together fragments of its dead results" (*PU*, p. 248). Through the process of living understanding individuals do more than respond to and reflect their environment. They become central to the process of creation itself. "What really *exists* is not things made but things in the making," he says. "Once made, they are dead, and an infinite number of alternative conceptual decompositions can be used in defining them. But put yourself *in the making* by a stroke of intuitive sympathy with the thing and, the whole range of possible decompositions coming at once into your possession, you are no longer troubled with the question which of them is the more absolutely true" (*PU*, p. 248).

James' view of experience provides an important life-enhancing contrast with philosophies of abstraction and death. It invests new power in the individual and moves the focus of philosophy from dead objects and ideas to growth and process. At the same time, by emphasizing the individual's freedom within a wider flux of experience, it also engages the reality of finitude and death. "Somewhere," says James, "being must immediately breast nonentity."[11] Concentrating on individual freedom, finitude, and independence from external standards, the self faces its own death and limitations as part of the process of growth. Anticipating modern existentialism, as Hoffman and others say, in a way that makes him startlingly relevant to contemporary thought, James understood that many people prefer a kind of death in life in a world with absolute answers to life's problems and moral dilemmas. People often choose illusions rather than painful realities, realities requiring faith in action and themselves.

Thus, James brilliantly discerned the powerful relationship between the fear of death and the unknown and the things in which we believe. The desire to overcome death helps maintain the resilience of the hold that absolute systems of truth have on many people. Just as the perverse self, in the stories of Poe and in the existentialism of Kierkegaard and Tillich, attempts to kill death through suicide, thus escaping the threat of death, the absolutist perverts the search for truth and the nature of experience by adopting absolute systems that incorporate disagreement, negation, and the unknown. In his essay on Hegel's method, James suggests that the dialectic involves such an attempt to find a death-killing absolute. He writes:

> Formally, this scheme of an organism of truth that has already fed as it were on its own liability to death, so that, death once dead for it, there's no more dying then, is the very fulfillment of the rationalistic aspiration. That one and only whole, with all its parts involved in it, negating and making one another impossible if abstracted and taken singly, but necessitating and holding one another in place if the whole of them be taken integrally, is the literal ideal sought after; it is the very diagram and picture of that notion of *the* truth with no outlying alternative, to which nothing can be added, nor from it anything withdrawn, and all variations from which are absurd, which so dominates the human imagination. (*PU*, p. 171)

Hegel's presentation of a determined and complete universe that incorporates death also eliminates for James the individual and freedom. A system that so neatly arrogates truth through abstraction also dissembles the basic process through which the individual operates "in the making" of experience and truth. For James, in the intellectual life of the mind as in the psychological domain of the self, the attempt to kill death produces sterility. From Hegel's model of the law of the heart—the perverted self in isolation from others because of the sense of moral superiority—we get to what James calls "this dumb region of the heart in which we dwell alone with our willingnesses and unwillingnesses, our faith and fears."[12] From the highly verbalistic and intellectualistic world of Hegel, we move to James' idea of an inner self of experience beyond words.

For James this humanistic understanding of experience invites a concomitant religious interpretation of experience. Instead of coming from an external absolute with divine powers, religion emerges from the experience of the self in the flow of life. Understanding aspects of experience as religious in turn feeds and strengthens the self as it contributes to the depth and power of the totality of human experience. Thus, in James the religious drive remains, as Quentin Anderson says, "confided to a new temple, the self." However, instead of immobilizing us, as Anderson also claims, for James the religious impulse sustains and even makes action possible in the practical world.

In fact, this impulse serves the most practical purpose of all in providing a positive answer to the question, "Is Life Worth Living?" In the essay by that name James confesses that only a belief in his own ability to provide life with meaning and to have an impact upon life makes the pain of life bearable. He writes: "Once more it is a case of *maybe*; and once more *maybes* are the essence of the situation. I confess that I do not see why the very existence of an invisible world may not in part depend on the personal response which any one of us may make to the religious appeal. God himself, in short, may draw vital strength and increase of very being from our fidelity."[13] Thus, James argues that only faith in an invisible world of higher meaning can make such a world happen and that only through making it happen can life seem worthwhile. He calls such beliefs faiths that verify themselves. "Now, in this description of faiths that verify themselves I have assumed that our faith in an invisible order is what inspires those efforts and that patience which make this visible order good for moral men." The alternative to faith in the invisible world is the "surrender to the nightmare view" that invites pessimism and suicide. But James' own understanding of experience makes the individual responsible for such nihilism. "This life," he writes, "*is* worth living, we can say, *since it is what we make it, from the moral point of view*; and we are determined to make it from that point of view, so far as we have anything to do with it, a success."[14]

In arguing that life divorced from ethical and moral considerations becomes worthless, James further argues that religious belief enables the individual to convert a sense of isolation and desperation into a source of spiritual energy for access to a higher world of ethical meaning. For James religious humanism preserves those very qualities of personal strength and action that comprise meaningful individualism. "You see now why I have been so individualistic throughout these lectures and why I have seemed so bent on rehabilitating the element of feeling in religion and subordinating its intellectual part," he writes in *The Varieties of Religious Experience*. "Individuality is founded in feeling; and the recesses of feeling, the darker, blinder strata of character, are the only places in the world in which we catch real fact in the making, and directly perceive how events happen, and how work is actually done. Compared with this world of living individualized feelings, the world of generalized objects which the intellect contemplates is without solidity or life."[15]

James maintains that the "ideal impulses" originate in "an altogether other dimension of existence from the sensible and merely 'understandable' world." He feels that we "belong" to this "other dimension" of experience "in a more intimate sense than that in which we belong to the visible world, for we belong in the most intimate sense wherever our ideals belong" (*VRE*, p. 506). Thus James, to use Quentin Anderson's terms, believes that the "visionary" dimension of life operates directly and immediately upon the "practical." In fact, he feels that the measure of the value of that higher life is derived from its consequences upon the individual and the way individuals act with each other. "Yet," he writes, "the unseen region in question is not merely ideal, for it produces effects in this world. When we commune with it, work is actually done upon our finite personality, for we are turned into new men, and consequences in the way of conduct follow in the natural world upon our regenerative change. But that which produces effects within another reality must be termed a reality itself, so I feel as if we had no philosophic excuse for calling the unseen or mystical world unreal" (*VRE*, pp. 506–507).

In accordance with this "thoroughly 'pragmatic' view of religion," James also argues that "God is real since he produces real effects" (*VRE*, pp. 508, 507). For James, of course, this is not the traditional monistic God but a more personal and individual "sort of polytheism" in which each person's God affects that person's life. People assume, says James, God "as a matter of course to be 'one and only' and to be 'infinite'; and the notion of many finite gods is one which hardly any one thinks it worthwhile to consider, and still less to uphold. Nevertheless, in the interests of intellectual clearness, I feel bound to say that religious experience, as we have studied it, cannot be cited as unequivocally supporting the infinitest belief. The only thing that it unequivocally testifies to is that we can experience union with *something* larger than ourselves and in that union find our greatest peace" (*VRE*, pp. 514–515). In order to have the power to change lives God, says James, "might conceivably even be only a larger and more godlike self, of which the present self would then be but the mutilated expression, and the universe might conceivably be a collection of such selves, of different degrees of inclusiveness, with no absolute unity realized in it at all" (*VRE*, p. 515). Based on the highly personal nature of religious experience, James suggests in his essay on Hegel that the real "enemy" of the God in which most people actually believe is the absolute picture of him that religions generally proffer. He writes, "Only thoroughgoing monists or pantheists believe in the absolute. The God of our popular Christianity is but one member of a pluralistic system. He and we stand outside of each other, just as the devil, the saints, and the angels stand outside of both of us. I can hardly conceive of anything more different from the absolute than the God, say, of David or of Isaiah" (*PU*, p. 174).

Ironically, such seemingly unconventional views about God in fact put James within a basic tradition in America which relates the innermost feelings and fears of individuals to their religious beliefs and practices. For example, in his study of the origins of American culture and character, Richard Slotkin compares the captivity myths of the Puritans to the terror sermons of Jonathan Edwards. Slotkin writes that "Jonathan Edwards's 'Sinners in the Hands of an Angry God' (1749)—the archetypal revival sermon by the most subtle student of the psychology of personal conversion—suggests the relevance of the captivity to the psychology of conversion."[16] Slotkin maintains that the precariousness of the individual in the captivity myth provides a model for the precariousness of the soul in the terror sermon. Accepting this interesting connection, one can see James' discussion of the self and religion as a modern version of the same story of the precariousness of the self. Soul and self, saintliness and sanity, intermingle in his ethical and religious writings. In the opening lines of "The Will to Believe," James says to his audience, "I have brought with me to-night something like a sermon on justification by faith to read to you—I mean an essay in justification *of* faith, a defence of our right to adopt a believing attitude in religious matters, in spite of the fact that our merely logical intellect may not have been coerced."[17]

Using a form and a terminology appropriate to his own time, James in effect rendered a message about psychological and spiritual survival. He lived through the last stages of what some critics and historians still call the country's age of innocence. Thus, his personal experience with darkness and despair still fell outside the basic national consciousness and experience. Although the world had changed, few were aware of the full significance of these changes. Today everyone knows. Therefore James' words may have a special compelling quality to us. His justification of belief amounts to a major response to the issues that such a contemporary sociologist and thinker as Daniel Bell sees as most crucial to our time. Bell writes: "The real problem of *modernity* is the problem of belief. To use an unfashionable term, it is a spiritual crisis, since the new anchorages have proved illusory and the old ones have become submerged. It is a situation which brings us back to nihilism; lacking a past or a future, there is only a void." He goes on to say, "What religion can restore is the continuity of generations, returning us to the existential predicaments which are the ground of humility and care for others. Yet such a continuity cannot be manufactured, nor a cultural revolution engineered. That thread is woven out of those experiences which give one a tragic sense of life, a life that is lived on the knife-edge of finitude and freedom."[18]

Of course, others besides James understood the complex relationship in modern culture among the paralysis of belief, the dissipation of the religious impulse, and the vitiation of the values of individualism. James, however, felt a special concern over the power of absolutes as palliatives for those who were most insecure over the crisis of belief. He felt that philosophies that create false absolutes to ease the pain of living, in Bell's phrase, "on the knife-edge of finitude and freedom" often influence in important ways the quality of life for people without ever facing serious pragmatic examination. Thus, for James such philosphies relate to neither humanism nor culture in any meaningful sense and also help put the realm of moral experience and ethics on an uncertain foundation. James clearly was frustrating for many in his own day and is for many in ours because he expressed without apology his belief in the importance of issues involving freedom, life, and moral action for which there are no final solutions. Yet his insistence on writing about these very issues when he could have concentrated on the search for new technologies of human behavior and social organization made him appear to some like an eccentric who belonged in another age.

More recently, James has been faulted for lacking enough sensitivity to the social and political needs of minorities and women, for espousing elitism along with educational reform, and for holding to his individualism when collective action was needed to create pressure for liberal and reform causes.[19] Such criticism certainly helps to balance our understanding of James' place in our history and to correct possible misconceptions that have arisen about him concerning his role as a crusader and reformer. We need to understand him in his entirety, not in terms of a romanticized ideal. However, measuring him against some sort of preconceived checklist of causes of and positions on current events can also lead to a superficial treatment of both James and those issues. While he was concerned about these social and political issues, his attention focused mostly on different problems and questions that were less fashionable and explosive. He was deeply concerned about finding a way to relate. the domain of the inner self and its sense of spiritual value to the world of action. He felt that without that connection life could not be meaningful. He therefore searched for, in Tolstoy's words, "the faith that gave the possibility of living" (*VRE*, p. 181). With this basic concern, he predicted that systems that ask for the surrender of individual freedom and selfhood would ultimately fail. Whatever their intention, their destruction of the inner life and the moral sphere would make their contributions impersonal, dehumanizing, and meaningless. Such understanding on his part leads me to believe that in his own day James spoke not only to the present but to the future and that the age in which he belongs is our own.

🎗 Chapter 10

After the sixties:
The continuing search

Images of the American self as perverted, inward turning, and isolated permeate our culture. Some would argue that the thrust toward equality accelerated by urbanization, technology, and the media furthers the perversion of the tradition of the pragmatic and autonomous self that William James and others proffer. At the very least, it is clear that an important relationship exists between radical individualism, radical egalitarianism, and the growth of an urban-based dynamic economy conducive to cultural diversity and upward mobility. Thus, in his study of authenticity and radical individualism in the modern age, Marshall Berman notes how all these concepts blend into and become a form of radical egalitarianism.[1] In this situation everyone's belief in their right to claim priority for their own needs and their own special qualities and interests can become what Eugene McCarthy describes as "the new equality," in which the old concept of equality of opportunity turns into the demand for absolute equality in economic, political, and cultural spheres. McCarthy warns that this trend will produce not a nation of autonomous and independent-minded individuals but a fragmented culture of isolated and insecure people. "The cultural security of Americans," he writes, "traditionally has been found in a society of some tension, but a society in which a balance between individual freedom and liberty on the one side and the social good on the other could be achieved. The alternative now offered, the security of equalization, is depersonalizing. It is a deceptively angelistic conception of man in society. It is one which cannot be sustained. It will in all likelihood move persons in search of security, if not identity, to accept greater and greater socialization in politics, in economics, and in culture."[2]

In recent fiction one of the most eloquent critics of the perversion of individualism has been Saul Bellow's Artur Sammler.

Sammler sees such individualism as an indulgence that opposes the dying humanistic and liberal tradition which he embodies as a remnant. A survivor of the worst of the Nazi regime, including the death of his wife and his own burial in a Nazi death ditch, Sammler senses the continued collapse of civilization in the hands of the war's victors. According to him, a cause of the general state of chaos resides in "the disease of the single self," a mass version of the perverse self existing in isolation without structure, discipline, or focus.[3] At one point in the novel, when Sammler is finally moved "to speak his mind," he concentrates on this one theme of the perversion of individualism and the self in contemporary culture (p. 226). He argues vehemently that "this liberation into individuality has not been a great success." He says:

> Now, as everyone knows, it has only been in the last two
> centuries that the majority of people in civilized countries
> have claimed the privilege of being individuals. Formerly they
> were slave, peasant, laborer, even artisan, but not person.
> It is clear that this revolution, a triumph for justice in many
> ways—slaves should be free, killing toil should end, the soul
> should have liberty—has also introduced new kinds of grief
> and misery, and so far, on the broadest scale, it has not been
> altogether a success. I will not even talk about the Communist
> countries, where the modern revolution has been most
> thwarted. To us the results are monstrous. Let us think only
> about our own part of the world. We have fallen into much
> ugliness. It is bewildering to see how much these new indi-
> viduals suffer, with their new leisure and liberty. (p. 228)

Sammler further believes that a meretricious creed of the "uniqueness of the soul" becomes in its popular form a tool for suppression (p. 229). By inculcating "a strange desire for originality," what Sammler calls "our modern individuality boom" encourages the development of a "theater of the soul" in which the "contrived individuality" of the characters ultimately becomes a universal death wish, "a peculiar longing for nonbeing" (pp. 229–235).

Given Sammler's moral character and intellectual authority, his arguments constitute a strong attack against the idea of radical individualism. He seems to argue that such individualism first enervates and then destroys the institutions of contemporary society. The prescience of his theories receive daily confirmation in his travels through New York City. Radical individualism, as he understands it, is a product of modern, urban society. As his nephew says, "Roots? Roots are not modern" (p. 245). Thus, the violence and the decay of the city are simply external forms of spiritual putrescence. "New York," Sammler says, "makes one think about the collapse of civilization, about Sodom and Gomorrah, the end of the world. The end wouldn't come as a surprise here. Many people already bank on it. And I don't know whether humankind is really all that much worse" (p. 304).

The concept of individualism that Sammler attacks so strongly emerges as the national ideal of the individual self in Michael Wood's study of images of American character and culture in Hollywood movies. "I want to suggest," writes Wood, "that there is in America a dream of freedom which appears in many places and many forms, which lies somewhere at the back of several varieties of isolationism and behind whatever we mean by individualism, which converts selfishness from something of a vice into something of a virtue, and which confers a peculiar, gleaming prestige on loneliness. It is a dream of freedom from others; it is a fear, to use a sanctioned and favorite word, of entanglement. It is what we mean when we say, in our familiar phrase, that we don't want to get involved." According to Wood, in several Hollywood movies "selfishness as a fierce moral ideal in its own right" becomes in fact "a plea for rampant, quirky orneriness, for the right of the individual to do exactly as he pleases."[4]

Obviously, to a considerable extent this image of the American self that Wood sees in the movies reflects a force within the culture. However, critics of the media are probably justified in seeing more than the mere mirroring of clear images that originate in American values and attitudes. As part of a vaster technological and communications system, Hollywood perpetuates perceptions of the American self. It does more than mirror reality—it helps reconstruct it according to a reality consistent with its own values and interests. This is how Marshall McLuhan, in his first studies of media, viewed the movies and Hollywood: as a force undermining traditional American values of individualism and subverting the character to sustain such values. In *The Mechanical Bride* (1951) he writes, "So Hollywood is like the ad agencies in constantly striving to enter and control the unconscious minds of a vast public, not in order to understand or to present these minds, as the serious novelist does, but in order to exploit them for profit."[5] During this stage of his thinking McLuhan, therefore, resembles other liberals of the period that we have discussed—

such as David Riesman, Erich Fromm, Lionel Trilling, and Henry Nash Smith—who expressed grave concern about the trends toward conformity and standardization of thought and life style. McLuhan, however, took as his special project the understanding and analysis of the media as an influence encouraging and forming American culture and character. Throughout *The Mechanical Bride* he contrasts a Thoreauvian vision of individualism and freedom with the materialism, conformity of thought and action, and standardization of life style that are promulgated by American mass media. Similarly, in "American Advertising," he sharply contrasts the Jeffersonian and Thoreauvian traditions of democracy with the developing totalitarianism of the media. Especially concerned about the "strong totalitarian squint—that of the social engineer"—and the "totalitarian techniques" of American market research as used by advertisers, McLuhan expressed the hope that "the energy which activates the ad-men" might someday "be transferred to the world of political speculation and creation" so that "America could still fulfill many of its broken Utopian promises, because its Jeffersonian tradition is still intact, and likewise its psychological vigour."[6]

However, a few years after writing these critical attacks on the media, McLuhan changed his approach in a way that symbolizes the evolution of radical consciousness and radical positions on culture from what originally had been liberal sentiments. Instead of attacking the media, McLuhan called for using the new technology of communications to alter the individual and culture. "When I wrote *The Mechanical Bride* some years ago," he says, "I did not realize that I was attempting a defense of book-culture against the new media. . . . What we have to defend today is not the values developed in any particular culture or by any one mode of communication. Modern technology presumes to attempt a total transformation of man and his environment."[7] In effect, through the force of the electronic media, McLuhan hoped to end the dichotomy within western thought and culture between the self and others and the individual and the masses. Previously, he says, the major figures in western thought separated over this dichotomy so that "Blake and the Romantics tended to devote themselves to one side of it, the mythic and collective," while "J. S. Mill, Matthew Arnold, and a great many others devoted themselves to the other side of the dilemma, the problem of individual culture and liberty in an age of mass-culture." McLuhan then asserts, "Our liberation from the dilemma may, as Joyce felt, come from the new electric technology, with its profound organic character. For the electric puts the mythic or collective dimensions of human experience fully into the conscious wake-a-day world."[8]

However, beneath this excitement concerning the media one senses the persistence of the old Thoreauvian values and message. Indeed, the image of the waking, which McLuhan of course relates to Joyce, can also be understood in Thoreau's terms of proposing "to brag as lustily as chanticleer in the morning, standing on his roost, if only to wake my neighbors up." For McLuhan's basic objective remains the old Thoreauvian-Whitmanesque ideal of the enlightened and creative individual who through her or his own poetic consciousness relates to and participates in a wider democratic culture. But, instead of using in a defensive manner the old literature and book mentality and technology to support individual selfhood and freedom, McLuhan decided to take an aggressive stand by using technology and the electric media to promulgate values of creativity and freedom. Thus, he hoped to deal with contemporary consciousness in terms and modes relevant to that consciousness.

There are, he maintains, interesting ironies in this history of the fight for individual selfhood. He argues that in the nineteenth century "western man fought the harder for individuality as he surrendered the idea of a unique personal existence. The nineteenth century artists made a mass-surrender of that unique selfhood, that had been taken for granted in the eighteenth century, as the new mass pressures made the burdens of selfhood too heavy."[9] For McLuhan the irony of this surrender of the unique self in the midst of a fight for individuality is not quite as great as the irony of the rediscovery of the self that he anticipates through the use of the new technology that many liberals feel indicates the doom of individuality. The new technology makes available to all the experience and the power of modernism which can liberate the individual self. "The art process," he writes, "had no sooner approached the rigorous, impersonal rationale of the industrial process, in the period from Poe to Valéry, than the assembly-line of symbolist art was transformed into the new 'stream of consciousness' mode of presentation. And the stream of consciousness is an open 'field' perception that reverses all aspects of the nineteenth century discovery of the assembly-line or of the 'technique' of invention." The revolution of sensibility occurred, he maintains, "when the consumer of popular art was invited by new art forms" to participate "in the art process itself." "This was the moment of transcendence of the Gutenberg technology," he writes. "The centuries-old separation of senses and functions ended in a quite unexpected unity."[10] For McLuhan, then, the electrification of modernism and traditional democratic values makes individual and cultural fulfillment and unity possible at last.

In retrospect one would seem justified in feeling that McLuhan's euphoria was somewhat premature. Perhaps McLuhan and the other prophets of technology succumbed too easily to a faith in new forces to make new connections and harmonies for individuals and for their relationship with culture. Left behind were many of the basic questions of the individual and self in a mass culture that were raised by liberals in the fifties and then forgotten in the excitement of the middle and late sixties. There was also a tendency to forget about the basic truth of the individual and the cultural costs of new technologies. For example, Morris Eaves describes such costs in terms of "translating" the principles of handwork into mechanized work. He says, "The basic issue might be clarified by noticing how the limitations of a familiar machine impose limitations on the user."[11] In the excitement that many expressed over the potential of the new technology, few considered the implications of exchanging one set of limitations for another. The cost to the self of technology and the imposition of requirements inherent in the processes and methods of what Jacques Ellul calls technique were overlooked. Thus, the myth of the infinite potential of technology and systems to solve problems led to a denigration of individual potential. Ironically, however, one could argue that any "miracles" in our political life and history have come less from technology and electricity than from more traditional sources of strength—what McLuhan in his earlier work called, in a very Thoreauvian fashion, one's inner resources. "We would do well," he says in *The Mechanical Bride*, "to strengthen those inner resources, which we still undoubtedly exert, to resist the mechanism of mass delirium and collective irrationalism."[12]

For Bellow's Sammler true individualism involves the organization and development of such inner resources for the purpose of maintaining one's sense of selfhood and integrity in relationship to one's culture and time. Thus, when asked to describe an alternative to the present abuses of individualism, Sammler says, "Perhaps the best is to have some order within oneself," (p. 228). For Sammler this idea of self-discipline entails a vital component of individualism that relates significantly to other important aspects of achieving a meaningful selfhood. He indicates that the creation of one's self cannot be divorced from the work that goes into that creation. Effort, pain, the idea of working in accordance with a notion of standards are means of imbuing value upon one's individuality and one's work that relate to the whole idea of creation itself. "When you know what pain is," says Sammler, "you agree that not to have been born is better. But being born one respects the powers of creation, one obeys the will of God— with whatever inner reservations truth imposes. As for duty— you are wrong. The pain of duty makes the creature upright, and this uprightness is no negligible thing. No, I stand by what I first said. There is also an instinct against leaping into Kingdom Come" (p. 220). Thus, Sammler refuses to forget the idea of the costs involved in his actions and his behavior. His individuality insists on his keeping track, like Thoreau, of the worth of things. This set of beliefs and values that relate to his concept of individuality actually serves to draw him out of himself. In contrast to earlier examples of the transcendence of the perverted self, Sammler's mind works in a pragmatic way that draws him out of himself to relate to complicated forms of experience and reality. "But individualism," he says, "is of no interest whatever if it does not extend truth. As personal distinction, enhancement, glory it is for me devoid of interest. I care for it only as an instrument for obtaining truth" (p. 234).

Sammler in effect offers a program for individualism that stands in strong contrast to the idea of "selfishness as a fierce moral ideal" which Michael Wood describes as so characteristic of America and which represents, for me, an extension of the perversion of the individualism of the Adamic hero who is isolated from others, his culture, and the best sense of himself. It is this idea of the self that Sammler sees as epidemic in New York, but it also relates to Lionel Trilling's understanding in *Sincerity and Authenticity* of certain forms of modern rebellion against so-called repressive standards of reality. Although concerned primarily about the receptivity among a "consequential part of the educated public" to the "doctrine that madness is health, that madness is liberation and authenticity," Trilling could also be thinking about the madness involved in the perverted self's retreat into the self for a false sense of security when he says, "The falsities of an alienated social reality are rejected in favour of an upward psychopathic mobility to the point of divinity, each one of us a Christ—

but with none of the inconveniences of undertaking to intercede, of being a sacrifice, of reasoning with rabbis, of making sermons, of having disciples, of going to weddings and to funerals, of beginning something and at a certain point remarking that it is finished." [13]

The history of this "upward psychopathic mobility" in the form of the perverted self that turns on itself in fear and hesitation and arrogance is extensive. It can be found in many of our most important literary and cultural figures discussed in this study. Basically, this is a movement to escape history by asserting one's freedom while abnegating responsibility for events and life. The inward turn of the perverted self therefore becomes a classic case of the kind of freedom that surrenders itself and identifies itself with forms of determinism and historical inevitability. However, for Isaiah Berlin the basic incompatibility of determinism and moral responsibility leads to the inseparability of freedom in any meaningful understanding of the word from the concept of moral responsibility. He writes, "The attempt, therefore, to shuffle off responsibility, which, at an empirical level, seems to rest upon this or that historical individual or society or set of opinions held or propagated by them, on to some metaphysical machinery which, because it is impersonal, excludes the very idea of moral responsibility, must always be invalid; and the desire to do so may, as often as not, be written down to the wish to escape from an' untidy, cruel, and above all seemingly purposeless world, into a realm where all is harmonious, clear, intelligible, mounting towards some perfect culmination which satisfies the demand of 'reason', or an aesthetic feeling, or a metaphysical impulse or religious craving; above all, where nothing can be the object of criticism or complaint or condemnation or despair." [14]

Significantly, in another essay Berlin further discusses this impulse to escape responsibility and history for an ideal world and relates it to "the creed of the solitary thinker," a creed that I consider to be a version of the perverted self. "I identify myself," he writes, "with my critical and rational moments. The consequences of my acts cannot matter, for they are not in my control; only my motives are. This is the creed of the solitary thinker who has defied the world and emancipated himself from the chains of men and things. In this form, the doctrine may seem primarily an ethical creed, and scarcely political at all; nevertheless, its political implications are clear, and it enters into the tradition of liberal individualism at least as deeply as the 'negative' concept of freedom." [15]

This image of the solitary thinker as an example of the perverted self stands in sharp contrast to the "American Scholar," whose duties, Emerson says, "are such as become Man Thinking. They may all be comprised in self-trust," he continues. "The office of the scholar is to cheer, to raise, and to guide men by showing them facts amidst appearances."[16] Through his description of this office, Emerson gives us what amounts to a creed of the American scholar that represents an important alternative to Berlin's outline of "the creed of the solitary thinker." Although independent and prepared to accept a state of solitude, Emerson's "Man Thinking" still sees himself as an intrinsic part of democratic culture. He operates as a cultural symbol of the American self that sustains the tradition of a pragmatic and humanistic individualism. Moreover, the pragmatism involved in Emerson's delineation of the scholar's duties and role anticipates William James, whose pragmatic humanism constitutes a moral challenge to those individuals who retreat within themselves and refuse to accept or acknowledge any responsibility for the consequences of their actions and beliefs. Indeed, James' insistence upon testing beliefs and actions in terms of their consequences helps define his pragmatism as a form of humanism. Noting from Charles Peirce that "beliefs are really rules for action," James describes "the pragmatic method" as the attempt "to interpret each notion by tracing its respective practical consequences." Each belief, he insists, "must run the gauntlet of all my other beliefs."[17]

Moreover, what James calls "this pragmatist talk about truths in the plural" further develops the American tradition of humanistic individualism in the very pluralistic terms that Berlin believes to be basic to any program capable of offering a meaningful alternative to what he sees as the totalitarian trend toward the perversion of "positive" liberty.[18] "Pluralism," Berlin writes, "with the measure of 'negative' liberty that it entails, seems to me a truer and more humane ideal than the goals of those who seek in the great, disciplined, authoritarian structures the ideal of 'positive' self-mastery by classes, or peoples, or the whole of mankind. It is truer, because it does, at least, recognize the fact that human goals are many, not all of them commensurable, and in perpetual rivalry with one another. To assume that all values can be graded on one scale, so that it is a mere matter of inspection to determine the highest, seems to me to falsify our knowledge that men are free agents, to represent moral decision as an operation which a slide-rule could, in principle, perform."[19] Understandably, Berlin's expectations for the future of individual liberty are pessimistic. "It may be," he writes, "that the ideal of freedom to choose ends without claiming eternal validity for them, and the pluralism of values connected with this, is only the late fruit of our declining capitalist civilization: an ideal which remote ages and primitive societies have not recognized, and one which posterity will regard with curiosity, even sympathy, but little comprehension."[20]

Of course, Berlin's sense of the diminishing possibility of realizing the ideal of freedom and individual liberty is clearly justified in terms of what appears to be the direction of social forces in contemporary culture as well as trends in social thought and analysis. At the same time, however, one can also argue that our strong literary and cultural tradition of pragmatic and humanistic individualism provides a foundation from which to work for a future that includes individual liberty as a major priority. At the heart of this tradition rests a belief in the importance of the moral dimension to the whole question of creating a democratic culture. As John Dewey says, "We have to see that democracy means the belief that humanistic culture *should* prevail; we should be frank and open in our recognition that the proposition is a moral one— like any idea that concerns what *should* be."[21]

In the debate during the past several decades over the best way to achieve this goal of a democratic culture, liberal groups have often found themselves at odds with more radical activitists and thinkers in a situation of cultural deadlock similar to the situation during the Transcendentalist period. Ironically, by themselves both sides often seem incomplete. The radical programs for individual transformation and cultural revolution of the sixties today seem basically naïve and, to some extent, even subversive of cultural and individual freedom. At the same time many of the old beliefs of traditional liberal reformism concerning the role and power of government and the government bureaucracy, the nature of humans in their relationship to culture, the potential of education and science for effecting progress, and the self-regulation of an open system of balances continue to need the critical reexamination forced upon them by various movements during recent years. Thus, the creation of a democratic culture may require the invention of a synthesis of both positions.

This need for continued invention falls within the basic tradition of American democracy. In the past the revolutionary inventiveness of democratic culture, as understood by those interested in what F. O. Matthiessen calls a literature and scholarship for

American democracy, did not demand the surrender of the life of the mind and of the individual self to the masses. However, to such exponents of this democratic tradition, the culture also could not allow the creation of unfair and artificial barriers that deny access to others and that create a false sense of superiority and value in the manner of the perverted self. As Dewey says, "The struggle for democracy has to be maintained on as many fronts as culture has aspects: political, economic, international, educational, scientific and artistic, religious." He goes on to add that under new conditions of history we now have to work for what had been "more or less a gift of grace." This new situation, he reminds us, "renders the problem a moral one to be worked out on moral grounds."[22] Those are precisely the grounds upon which the American self stands best. Such moral grounds form the basis of our individuality and earned sense of selfhood. They will continue to be the only grounds upon which a meaningful American self can stand in the future.

Notes

1. The Modern Tradition and the American Self: Individualism and the Perverted Self

1. Irving Howe, "Introduction: The Idea of the Modern," in *Literary Modernism*, ed. Irving Howe (New York: Fawcett, 1967), pp. 12–13. Also see Howe's *Decline of the New* (New York: Horizon Press, 1970).
2. Richard Ellmann and Charles Feidelson, Jr., eds., *The Modern Tradition: Backgrounds of Modern Literature* (New York: Oxford University Press, 1965), p. v.
3. Ihab Hassan, *Radical Innocence: The Contemporary American Novel* (New York: Harper Colophon, 1961), pp. 9, 32. For related studies see also Eugene Goodheart, *The Cult of the Ego: The Self in Modern Literature* (Chicago: University of Chicago Press, 1968), and Raymond M. Olderman, *Beyond the Waste Land: The American Novel in the Nineteen-Sixties* (New Haven: Yale University Press, 1972).
4. Hassan, *Radical Innocence*, p. 33.
5. Paul de Man, *Blindness and Insight: Essays in the Rhetoric of Contemporary Criticism* (New York: Oxford University Press, 1971), p. 8.
6. Ibid., p. 19.
7. Ibid., pp. 142, 147, 148, 152, 151.
8. What de Man says about the value of modernity as a method for studying and reading literature can apply to American culture as a whole: "Modernity turns out to be indeed one of the concepts by means of which the distinctive nature of literature can be revealed in all its intricacy" (*Blindness and Insight*, p. 161).
9. Frederick J. Hoffman, "William James and the Modern Literary Consciousness," *Criticism* 4 (Winter 1962): 1–13. See also Hoffman's *The Mortal No: Death and the Modern Imagination* (Princeton: Princeton University Press, 1964).
10. Frederick J. Hoffman, "Freedom and Conscious Form: Henry James and the American Self," *Virginia Quarterly Review* 37 (Spring 1967): 269, 271.
11. Richard Poirier, *A World Elsewhere: The Place of Style in American*

Literature (Oxford: Oxford University Press, 1966), pp. 5, 7, 5, 9.

12. Sacvan Bercovitch, *The Puritan Origins of the American Self* (New Haven: Yale University Press, 1975), pp. 137, 151–152, 151.

13. See Poirier, *World Elsewhere*, pp. 9, 17, 35.

14. Dwight Macdonald, "Masscult & Midcult," in his *Against the American Grain: Essays on the Effects of Mass Culture* (New York: Vintage, 1962), pp. 20, 56.

15. Lawrence Buell, *Literary Transcendentalism: Style and Vision in the American Renaissance* (Ithaca: Cornell University Press, 1973), pp. 272, 273, notes that for the Transcendentalists "democratic individualism" was confusing because "their notion of the dignity of the individual was conditioned by an elitist upbringing (either moral elitism or social elitism or both), which also made them feel threatened by 'the people' or 'the great mass' as an actual force."

16. David Riesman, "The Saving Remnant: An Examination of Character Structure," in his *Individualism Reconsidered* (New York: Free Press, 1954), p. 118.

17. Louis Hartz, "The New Individualism and the Progressive Tradition," in *Innocence and Power: Individualism in Twentieth-Century America*, ed. Gordon Mills (Austin: University of Texas Press, 1965), p. 72.

18. Theodore Dreiser, "The Myth of Individuality," *The American Mercury* 31 (March 1934): 337–338, writes: "It is only as a fraction of a multitude such as a race that he is able to exist as a so-called unit. No race, no man. It is not the man that is living, but the race or races and their creative chemisms. Man is not living, but is being lived by something which needs not only him but billions like him in order to express itself. What that something is, he has never been able to discover. Hence, the complete lack of individuality of the so-called individual."

19. Frederick J. Hoffman, "Dogmatic Innocence: Self-Assertion in Modern American Literature," in *Innocence and Power*, p. 116.

20. Quentin Anderson, *The Imperial Self: An Essay in American Literary and Cultural History* (New York: Vintage, 1971), pp. 21, 39, 40, 4.

21. Bercovitch, *Puritan Origins of the American Self*, p. 166. Bercovitch further states, "Emerson's sources for this *emergent* allegory of history were the writings of his colonial forebears. He acknowledged them proudly, as a spiritual tribute. . . . Emerson's project is outlined in his essays and journals from the 1830s through the Civil War. The 'two great epochs of public principle' were for him 'the Planting, and the Revolution of the colony.' 'The new is only the seed of the old,' he wrote in 1841. 'What is this abolition and non-resistance . . . but a continuation of Puritanism. . . ?'"

22. See Albert William Levi, "The Value of Freedom: Mill's Liberty," in *Ethics* 70 (October 1959): 37–46; rpt. in John Stuart Mill, *On Liber-*

ty, ed. David Spitz, Norton Critical Edition (New York: Norton, 1975), p. 194.

23. Levi writes that "just as there must be freedom of self-determination for the inner life, so there must be freedom for public discussion and deliberation about outward acts. Selves are largely formed and continually remade in the process of interacting with their fellows, and the very formation of responsible selves *requires* that they speak freely, respond to the words of others, develop the latent powers of their reason by testing the alternatives before them. For however the self is a social emergent, growing out of a prior social environment, *selfhood is axiologically prior to society*, and society must respect individuality in its own nature as the source of all values" (ibid., pp. 194–195).

24. Isaiah Berlin, *Four Essays on Liberty* (London: Oxford University Press, 1969), p. lvii.

25. Ibid., p. xlv.

26. Ibid., pp. xlvi–xlvii.

27. Ibid., pp. 135, 136.

28. G. W. F. Hegel, *The Phenomenology of Mind*, trans. J. B. Baillie, introduction by George Lichtheim, Torchbook Edition (New York: Harper Colophon, 1967), pp. 391, 393.

29. Ibid., p. 396.

30. Ernst Cassirer, *The Myth of the State* (New Haven: Yale University Press, 1946), p. 257.

31. Thomas Jefferson to Isaac H. Tiffany, April 4, 1819, in *The Political Writings of Thomas Jefferson: Representative Selections*, ed. Edward Dumbauld (Indianapolis: Bobbs-Merrill, 1955), p. 55.

32. Jefferson to Francis W. Gilmer, June 7, 1816, in *Political Writings*, p. 55.

33. Jefferson to William S. Smith, November 13, 1787, in *Political Writings*, p. 68.

34. James Madison, no. 51 in *The Federalist Papers*, introduction by Clinton Rossiter (New York: Mentor, 1961), pp. 325, 322.

35. See John Dewey, "The Lost Individual," in his *Individualism Old and New* (1929; rpt. New York: Capricorn, 1962), p. 56.

36. Irving Howe, "Anarchy and Authority in American Literature," in his *Decline of the New*, p. 102.

37. See John William Ward's afterword to Cooper's *The Prairie* (New York: Signet, 1964), pp. 403–411.

38. D. H. Lawrence, *Studies in Classic American Literature* (1923; rpt. Garden City: Doubleday Anchor, 1951), pp. 64, 59, 72–73, 72.

39. See Henry Nash Smith in the introduction to Cooper's *The Prairie* (New York: Rinehart Edition, 1950), p. xviii.

40. James Fenimore Cooper, *The Deerslayer* (New York: Washington Square Press, 1964), p. 35. All subsequent references to this novel

will be to this edition and will be included parenthetically in the text.

41. R. W. B. Lewis, *The American Adam* (Chicago: University of Chicago Press, 1955), pp. 104, 104–105, 105.
42. Georg Lukács, "The Ideology of Modernism," in his *Realism in Our Time* (1958; rpt. New York: Harper Torchbook Edition, 1971), p. 20.
43. Lewis, *American Adam*, p. 5.
44. Lukács, "Ideology of Modernism," p. 21.
45. Ibid., pp. 22, 23, 24, 26, 24.
46. See Henry Nash Smith, *Virgin Land: The American West as Symbol and Myth* (1950; rpt. Cambridge, Mass.: Harvard University Press, 1973).
47. Richard Slotkin, *Regeneration through Violence: The Mythology of the American Frontier, 1600–1860* (Middletown, Conn.: Wesleyan University Press, 1973), p. 557.

2. Poe and the Transcendent Self

1. Lionel Trilling, *The Liberal Imagination: Essays on Literature and Society* (1949; rpt. New York: Charles Scribner's Sons, 1976), p. xi.
2. Trilling provides the following interesting if all-inclusive definition of culture consistent with these remarks about politics and culture in *Beyond Culture: Essays on Literature and Learning* (New York: Viking, 1965), p. xi: "If one speaks of the tendency toward homogeneity in modern culture, one is necessarily implicated in the semantic difficulties of the word *culture*. These are notorious. Everyone is conscious of at least two meanings of the word. One of them refers to that complex of activities which includes the practice of the arts and of certain intellectual disciplines, the former being more salient than the latter. It is this meaning that we have in mind when we talk about popular culture as distinguished from 'high' culture, or about Ministry of Culture, or about the cultural attaché of an embassy. The other meaning is much more inclusive. It comprises a people's technology, its manners and customs, its religious beliefs and organization, its systems of valuation, whether expressed or implicit. (If the people in question constitutes a highly developed modern nation, its social organization and its economy are usually excluded from the concept of culture and considered separately, although the reciprocal influence of social-economic and cultural factors are of course taken into account.) When the word is used in the second and larger sense, the extent of its reference includes a people's art and thought, but only as one element among others. The two meanings of the word, so different in their scope, permit us to say—it is a dubious privilege—that a certain culture sets a higher store by culture than does some other culture."

3. Richard Wilbur, introduction to Edgar Allan Poe in *Major Writers of America*, ed. Perry Miller, 2 vols. (New York: Harcourt, Brace & World, 1962), I, 378.

4. Most of these critics seem to accept with qualification and go beyond the classic psychoanalytical approach in Marie Bonaparte, *The Life and Works of Edgar Allan Poe: A Psychoanalytic Study* (London: Imago, 1949). See also Patrick F. Quinn, *The French Face of Edgar Poe* (Carbondale: Southern Illinois University Press, 1957); Harry Levin, *The Power of Blackness* (New York: Vintage, 1960); Thomas F. Walsh, "The Other William Wilson," *American Transcendental Quarterly* 10 (Spring 1971): 17–26; Roy Male, introduction to Edgar Allan Poe in *American Literary Masters*, ed. Charles R. Anderson et al., 2 vols. (New York: Holt, Rinehart and Winston, 1965), I, 3–18; David Halliburton, *Edgar Allan Poe: A Phenomenological View* (Princeton: Princeton University Press, 1973); David H. Hirsch, "The Pit and the Apocalypse," *Sewanee Review* 76 (Autumn 1968): 632–652; Robert Shulman, "Poe and the Powers of the Mind," *Journal of English Literary History* 37 (June 1970): 245–262; and Arthur Lerner, *Psychoanalytically Oriented Criticism of Three American Poets: Poe, Whitman and Aiken* (Rutherford, N.J.: Fairleigh Dickinson University Press, 1970).

5. R. D. Laing, *The Divided Self: An Existential Study in Sanity and Madness* (1960; rpt. Baltimore: Penguin, 1965), p. 17. All subsequent references will be to this edition and will be included parenthetically in the text as *TDS*.

6. Quinn, "That Spectre in My Path," *French Face of Edgar Poe*, p. 244.

7. Edgar Allan Poe, "The Fall of the House of Usher," in *Selected Writings*, ed. Edward H. Davidson (Boston: Houghton Mifflin, 1956), p. 95. All subsequent references to Poe's stories will be to this edition and will be included parenthetically in the text.

8. Richard Wilbur, "The House of Poe," in *Poe: A Collection of Critical Essays*, ed. Robert Regan (Englewood Cliffs, N.J.: Prentice-Hall, 1967), p. 108.

9. See also Wilbur's interpretation of the house in ibid., p. 110.

10. Joseph J. Moldenhauer, "Murder as a Fine Art: Basic Connections between Poe's Aesthetics, Psychology, and Moral Vision," *P.M.L.A.* 83 (May 1968): 295.

11. Ibid.

12. Sören Kierkegaard, *Either/Or: A Fragment of Life*, trans. David F. Swenson, Lillian Marvin Swenson, and Walter Lowrie, in *A Kierkegaard Anthology*, ed. Robert Bretall (New York: Modern Library, 1946), p. 38.

13. G. R. Thompson, "Unity, Death, and Nothingness—Poe's 'Romantic Skepticism,'" *P.M.L.A.* 85 (March 1970): 299, says of "The Pit and the Pendulum": "The horror of horrors, which Poe leaves purposely unstated and which so appalls the narrator of 'The Pit and the Pendu-

lum,' is the same unknown yet half-known Nothingness, lurking at the bottom of the pit (like darkness over the waters in Genesis)."

14. Walsh, "The Other William Wilson," p. 24, says, "Wilson's double represents the ego ideal and the conscience."

15. Charles Baudelaire, "New Notes on Edgar Poe," in *The Recognition of Edgar Allan Poe: Selected Criticism since 1829*, ed. Eric W. Carlson (Ann Arbor: University of Michigan Press, 1966), p. 47.

16. Paul Tillich, *The Courage To Be* (New Haven: Yale University Press, 1952), p. 66.

17. Ibid., p. 75.

18. Kierkegaard, *The Sickness unto Death*, trans. Walter Lowrie, in *A Kierkegaard Anthology*, p. 342.

19. Hirsch, "The Pit and the Apocalypse," p. 637, relates this story to Kierkegaard. For another discussion of Poe and Kierkegaard see Quinn, *French Face of Edgar Poe*, pp. 160, 166.

20. R. D. Laing, *The Politics of Experience* (New York: Ballantine, 1967), p. 133.

21. Ibid., pp. 115, 75, 74.

22. Thompson, "Unity, Death, and Nothingness—Poe's 'Romantic Skepticism,'" p. 300.

23. See Lionel Trilling, *Sincerity and Authenticity* (Cambridge, Mass.: Harvard University Press, 1972), pp. 159–161.

3. Emerson and Brownson: The Scholar, the Self, and Society

1. Bercovitch, *Puritan Origins of the American Self*, p. 165.

2. Buell, *Literary Transcendentalism*, p. 282.

3. Perry Miller, ed., *The American Transcendentalists: Their Prose and Poetry* (New York: Anchor, 1957), p. x.

4. Perry Miller, ed., *The Transcendentalists: An Anthology* (Cambridge, Mass.: Harvard University Press, 1950), p. 12. All subsequent quotations from this anthology will be included parenthetically in the text.

5. Buell, *Literary Transcendentalism*, p. 8.

6. Buell says, "Altogether, the Transcendentalist movement was more an evolution than a revolt from Unitarianism, although there were also basic philosophical differences that should not be glossed over. Transcendentalism was in almost every way a logical end result of the momentum of the Unitarian movement, just as liberalism has led to radicalism in the moral thought of the last two decades" (ibid., p. 38).

7. See Henry Nash Smith, "The American Scholar Today," *Southwest Review* 48 (Summer 1963): 191–199; rpt. in *"The American Scholar" Today: Emerson's Essay and Some Critical Views*, ed. C. David Mead (New York: Dodd, Mead & Co., 1970), p. 69. See also Smith's "Emerson's Problem of Vocation: A Note on the American Scholar," *The New England Quarterly* 12 (March 1939): 52–67; rpt. in *Amer-*

ican Transcendentalism: An Anthology of Criticism, ed. Brian M. Barbour (Notre Dame: University of Notre Dame Press, 1973), pp. 225–237.

8. Smith, "The American Scholar Today," p. 69.
9. Ibid., pp. 76–77.
10. Ibid., p. 77.
11. Trilling, *Liberal Imagination*, p. 88.
12. For a collection of essays by such liberal thinkers who were critical of conforming aspects of the culture of the 1950s, see *Mass Culture: The Popular Arts in America*, ed. Bernard Rosenberg and David Manning White (New York: Free Press, 1957).
13. Trilling, *Sincerity and Authenticity*, p. 164.
14. See A. Robert Caponigri, "Brownson and Emerson: Nature and History," *The New England Quarterly* 18 (September 1945): 368–390; rpt. in *American Transcendentalism*, pp. 239–256. See also Gustaaf Van Cromphout, "Emerson and the Dialectics of History," *P.M.L.A.* 91 (January 1976): 54–65.
15. Quoted in Buell, *Literary Transcendentalism*, p. 41.
16. For an interesting critical debate over the meaning of "Literary Ethics" and the reaction to it, see Merton M. Sealts, Jr., "Emerson on the Scholar, 1838: A Study of 'Literary Ethics,'" in *Literature and Ideas in America: Essays in Memory of Henry Hayden Clark*, ed. Robert Falk (Athens: Ohio University Press, 1975), pp. 52–53, and Joel Porte, *Emerson and Thoreau: Transcendentalists in Conflict* (Middletown, Conn.: Wesleyan University Press, 1966), pp. 22, 23.
17. Bercovitch, *Puritan Origins of the American Self*, pp. 174–175, says, "Emerson's hero, like Mather's Winthrop, derives his greatness from the enterprise he represents. Despite his distaste for, and fear of, the mass of actual Americans, he did not need to dissociate himself from America because he had already dissociated the mass from the American idea."
18. Americo D. Lapati, introduction to *The American Republic: Its Constitution, Tendencies and Destiny*, by Orestes Brownson (New Haven: College and University Press, 1972), pp. 10–11.
19. Brownson, *The American Republic*, p. 60.
20. Brownson eventually turned from radicalism to a concept of Christian liberty. In "Socialism and the Church," in *Orestes Brownson: Selected Essays*, ed. Russell Kirk (New York: Gateway, 1955), pp. 101–102, he says: "Socialism, by its very principle, enslaves us to nature and society, and subjects us to all the fluctuations of time and sense. According to it, man can attain to true good, can gain the end for which he was made, only in a certain political and social order, which it depends on the millions, whom the individual cannot control, to construct, and which, when constructed, may prove to be inconvenient and inadequate, and require to be pulled down and built up again. The individual, it teaches us, can make no advance

towards his destiny but in proportion as he secures the cooperation of his race. All men must be brought down or brought up to the same level before he can go to the end for which his God made him; each man's true good is unattainable, till all men are prepared to take 'a pull, a strong pull, a long pull, and a pull together,' to attain theirs! This is slavery, not liberty. Nay, it denies the possibility of liberty, and makes slavery the condition of all men."

21. Anderson, *Imperial Self*, pp. 236, 41.
22. See James M. Cox, "R. W. Emerson: The Circles of the Eye," in *Emerson: Prophecy, Metamorphosis, and Influence*, Selected Papers from the English Institute, ed. David Levin (New York: Columbia University Press, 1975), pp. 76–81. See also Maurice Gonnaud, "Emerson and the Imperial Self: A European Critique," in the same volume, pp. 108, 127.
23. Hoffman, "Dogmatic Innocence," pp. 114, 116–117.
24. Bercovitch, *Puritan Origins of the American Self*, pp. 173, 178.
25. Ibid., p. 168.
26. Ralph Waldo Emerson, "The American Scholar," in *The Complete Works of Ralph Waldo Emerson*, ed. Edward Waldo Emerson, 12 vols. (Boston: Houghton Mifflin, 1903–1904), I, 101–102. All subsequent references to this essay will be from this edition and will be included parenthetically in the text.
27. F. O. Matthiessen, *American Renaissance: Art and Expression in the Age of Emerson and Whitman* (London: Oxford University Press, 1941), p. xv.

4. Whitman: Culture and Self

1. Edwin Haviland Miller, "The Radical Vision of Whitman and Pollock," in *The Artistic Legacy of Walt Whitman: A Tribute to Gay Wilson Allen*, ed. Edwin Haviland Miller (New York: New York University Press, 1970), p. 55.
2. Robert Duncan, "Changing Perspectives in Reading Whitman," in *Artistic Legacy of Walt Whitman*, p. 73.
3. Ibid.
4. Harold Kaplan, *Democratic Humanism and American Literature* (Chicago: University of Chicago Press, 1972), pp. 201–202, says on this issue of dialectic in Whitman that "like Emerson, Whitman pursued unity and found dialectic on his way. Whether one stressed conflict or compensation, the thinking conceived opposite values and accepted antithesis in the nature of things. The purpose of the mind was synthesis, but meanwhile the real health of the moral sensibility was indicated in the acceptance of pluralist and combative terms."
5. Eugene Goodheart, *Culture and the Radical Conscience* (Cambridge, Mass.: Harvard University Press, 1973), p. 1.

6. Hayden White, "The Culture of Criticism," in *Liberations: New Essays on the Humanities in Revolution*, ed. Ihab Hassan (Middletown, Conn.: Wesleyan University Press, 1971), p. 62.

7. See George Santayana, "The Poetry of Barbarism," in his *Interpretations of Poetry and Religion* (1900; rpt. Gloucester: Peter Smith, 1969), pp. 166–187.

8. White, "The Culture of Criticism," p. 67.

9. Ibid., p. 57. Similarly, George Steiner in *In Bluebeard's Castle* (New Haven: Yale University Press, 1971), pp. 91, 81, believes that "particularly in the United States some fashionable, silly theories about total revolutions of consciousness" contribute to "the collapse, more or less complete, more or less conscious," of the "agreed hierarchic value-structure" that formed western culture. Also Goodheart, *Culture and the Radical Conscience*, p. 31, says, "What has been distressing about the current cultural radicalism in America is that it has joined up without knowing it with the dominant philistine resentment toward intellectual and artistic culture."

10. White, "The Culture of Criticism," p. 67.

11. Ibid., p. 68.

12. Kaplan, *Democratic Humanism and American Literature*, pp. 7–8, says, "As Tocqueville understood, the key to the American moral and philosophic imagination lay in the historic elimination of hierarchical structures. Egalitarian principles opposed themselves to the hierarchical metaphysics of heaven and earth, of gods, angels and men, and to the hierarchies of society for rank, trade and class. Class and degree in ideas, in values, ultimately in the distinction between good and evil and between salvation and damnation, would finally be threatened in the extreme secularization of thought to which Emerson and Whitman carried the premises of democracy."

13. Richard Chase, *Walt Whitman Reconsidered* (New York: William Sloane, 1955), p. 153. Chase and many others discuss the sources of Whitman's political, social, and economic beliefs. See Newton Arvin, *Whitman* (New York: Macmillan, 1938), and Gay Wilson Allen, *The Solitary Singer*, rev. ed. (1955; rpt. New York: New York University Press, 1967). For a recent discussion of the influence of the democratic modern self in Whitman, see Richard J. Fein, "Whitman and the Emancipated Self," *The Centennial Review* 20 (Winter 1976): 36–49.

14. Santayana, "The Poetry of Barbarism," pp. 181, 180.

15. Gay Wilson Allen, *A Reader's Guide to Walt Whitman* (New York: Farrar, Straus & Giroux, 1970), p. 159.

16. David Daiches, "Walt Whitman: Impressionist Prophet," in *Leaves of Grass: One Hundred Years After*, ed. Milton Hindus (Stanford: Stanford University Press, 1955), p. 116.

17. Walt Whitman, *Democratic Vistas*, in *Complete Poetry and Selected Prose*, ed. James E. Miller, Jr. (Boston: Houghton Mifflin, 1959), p.

476. All subsequent references to Whitman's poetry and prose, unless otherwise noted, will be to this edition and will be included parenthetically in the text.

18. Muriel Rukeyser, "Backgrounds and Sources," in *A Century of Whitman Criticism*, ed. Edwin Haviland Miller (Bloomington: Indiana University Press, 1969), p. 193.

19. Gay Wilson Allen, "Introduction to Walt Whitman's Poems," in *A Century of Whitman Criticism*, p. 327. See also John B. Mason, "Walt Whitman's Catalogues: Rhetorical Means for Two Journeys in 'Song of Myself,'" *American Literature* 45 (March 1973): 48, 49.

20. George Steiner, *Language and Silence: Essays on Language, Literature and the Inhuman* (New York: Atheneum, 1972), p. 27.

21. Steiner, *In Bluebeard's Castle*, pp. 113–114.

22. See Kaplan, *Democratic Humanism and American Literature*, p. 208.

23. See Edwin H. Miller, *Walt Whitman's Poetry: A Psychoanalytic Journey* (New York: New York University Press, 1968), p. 174.

24. Norman O. Brown, *Life against Death: The Psychoanalytic Meaning of History* (New York: Vintage, 1959), pp. 309, 137–176, 202–223, 307–322.

25. Ibid., p. 309.

26. Ibid., p. 308.

27. See also John F. Lynen, *The Design of the Present: Essays on Time and Form in American Literature* (New Haven: Yale University Press, 1969), pp. 318–322, for another discussion of death and time in Whitman's poetry.

28. Whitman to Emerson, August 1856, in *Leaves of Grass*, ed. Sculley Bradley and Harold W. Blodgett, Norton Critical Edition (New York: Norton, 1973), pp. 739–740.

29. Brown, *Life against Death*, p. 311.

30. Ibid., pp. 150–151.

31. Goodheart, *Culture and the Radical Conscience*, p. 25.

32. David Daiches, "Politics and the Literary Imagination," in *Liberations*, pp. 103, 107.

33. F. O. Matthiessen, *American Renaissance*, pp. 546, 367. Also, J. Middleton Murry, "Walt Whitman: The Prophet of Democracy," in *Leaves of Grass: One Hundred Years After*, p. 127, says that "behind and beneath Whitman's promulgation of his total self as a type of the citizen of the ideal Democracy is a deeply religious humility. Unless his 'egotism' is apprehended against this background of religion it is bound to be misunderstood." Newton Arvin, *Whitman*, p. 289, argues that "what is weakly transcendental or too simply egoistic or waywardly personal" in Whitman finds opposition in his larger achievement of giving utterance to that which is "profoundly progressive, profoundly humanistic."

34. Chase, *Walt Whitman Reconsidered*, p. 155.

35. Matthew Arnold, *Culture and Anarchy*, ed. J. Dover Wilson (Cambridge, Eng.: Cambridge University Press, 1966), p. 70.
36. Ibid., pp. 70, 69.
37. Whitman in *Democratic Vistas*, p. 497, called aesthetic value the major determinant in considering works "first-class" but "then, whenever claiming to be first-class works, they are to be strictly and sternly tried by their foundation in, and radiation, in the highest sense and always indirectly, of, the ethic principles and eligibility to free, arouse, dilate."
38. Walt Whitman, *The Eighteenth Presidency*, ed. Edward F. Grier (Lawrence: University of Kansas Press, 1956), p. 34.
39. Ibid., p. 35.
40. Ibid.
41. Ibid., pp. 28, 24, 23, 26.
42. Ibid., p. 39.
43. William James, "The Will to Believe," in *Essays on Faith and Morals*, ed. Ralph Barton Perry (1942; rpt. New York: Meridian, 1962), p. 56.

5. Howells: The Rebel in the One-Dimensional Age

1. Edwin H. Cady in *The Road to Realism: The Early Years 1837–1885 of William Dean Howells* (Syracuse: Syracuse University Press, 1956), p. 211, and William M. Gibson, ed., in Howells' *A Modern Instance* (Boston: Houghton Mifflin, 1957), p. xvi, tend to agree with an early *Atlantic* review of the novel by Horace E. Scudder, who said it was "a demonstration of a state of society of which the divorce laws are the index." Lionel Trilling, "William Dean Howells," in his *The Opposing Self: Nine Essays in Criticism* (New York: Viking, 1955), p. 82, calls Bartley "the quintessence of the average sensual man." Although seeing some good traits in Bartley, Olov W. Fryckstedt, in *In Quest of America: A Study of Howells' Early Development as a Novelist* (Uppsala, 1958), p. 237, says, "Bartley Hubbard was Howells' most pessimistic estimate of the average American." James W. Gargano, in "*A Modern Instance*: The Twin Evils of Society," *Texas Studies in Literature and Language* 4 (Autumn 1962): 400, calls Bartley the exemplification of the "middle class American without traditions to guide him in his competitive quest for recognition."
2. William McMurray, *The Literary Realism of William Dean Howells* (Carbondale: Southern Illinois University Press, 1967), p. 42. Gargano, in spite of his association of Bartley with the middle class, has also called him "the rather gay moth who threatens to destroy the social fabric" ("*A Modern Instance*: The Twin Evils of Society," p. 399).

3. William Dean Howells, *A Modern Instance*, ed. William M. Gibson (Boston: Houghton Mifflin, 1957), pp. 356, 270. Subsequent references to this work will be to this edition and will be made parenthetically in the text.

4. The Squire's character and the significance of his place in the novel for the other characters have been the subject of interesting commentary. Kermit Vanderbilt argues in *The Achievement of William Dean Howells: A Reinterpretation* (Princeton: Princeton University Press, 1968), pp. 64–75, that Marcia had an Electra complex. This condition would certainly add to the intense nature of the Squire's relationship with her suitor, Bartley. George N. Bennett, in *William Dean Howells: The Development of a Novelist* (Norman: University of Oklahoma Press, 1959), p. 120, argues that it is not until the end of the novel that "the virus of moral corruption has infected Squire Gaylord." I think, however, that the origins of that virus are apparent from the beginning. Thomas F. Walsh, in "Howells' *A Modern Instance*," *The Explicator* 23 (April 1965): item 59, likens the Squire to a "Hawthornean devil" who delegates himself the power of divine retribution.

5. Gibson, in Howells' *A Modern Instance*, p. xi.

6. Hassan, *Radical Innocence*, p. 44.

7. Ibid., pp. 44, 33.

8. Ibid., p. 44.

9. Samuel L. Clemens to Howells, July 24, 1882, in *Mark Twain–Howells Letters: The Correspondence of Samuel L. Clemens and William Dean Howells, 1872–1910*, ed. Henry Nash Smith and William M. Gibson, 2 vols. (Cambridge, Mass.: Harvard University Press, 1960), I, 412. Also see Howells' letter to Brander Matthews, July 22, 1911, in *Life in Letters of William Dean Howells*, ed. Mildred Howells, 2 vols. (Garden City: Doubleday, Doran, 1928), II, 301.

10. Kenneth S. Lynn, *William Dean Howells: An American Life* (New York: Harcourt Brace Jovanovich, 1971), calls Howells a modern consciousness but concentrates on Howells as an artist. See also William M. Gibson's review of *The Achievement of William Dean Howells*, by Kermit Vanderbilt, *American Literature* 44 (May 1972): 327–328. For an invaluable survey of recent Howells scholarship, especially of studies that develop the theme of his modernity, see Kermit Vanderbilt, "Howells Studies: Past, or Passing, or to Come," *American Literary Realism 1870–1910* 7 (Spring 1974): 143–153.

11. New York *Herald*, September 23, 1894, sec. 6, p. 7. This anonymous article and a second one that appeared in the New York *Daily Tribune*, September 30, 1894, are discussed by Clara Marburg Kirk in *W. D. Howells, Traveler from Altruria, 1889–1894* (New Brunswick: Rutgers University Press, 1962), pp. 97–98. For a complete bibliography of articles discussing the sources and nature of Howells' political, social, and economic thought, see James L. Woodress and

Stanley P. Anderson, "A Bibliography of Writing about William Dean Howells," *American Literary Realism 1870–1910*, special number (1969), and Ulrich Halfmann and Don R. Smith, "William Dean Howells: A Revised and Annotated Bibliography of Secondary Comment in Periodicals and Newspapers, 1868–1919," *American Literary Realism 1870–1910* 5 (Spring 1972): 91–121. See also Daniel Aaron's important discussion of Howells in terms of his place in the American progressive tradition in *Men of Good Hope: A Story of American Progressives* (London: Oxford University Press, 1951).

12. Howells to Henry James, October 10, 1888, in *Life in Letters*, I, 417. Howells was capable of laughing at his own pessimism. In a later letter he said that both he and Mark Twain deserved the epithet "theoretical socialists and practical aristocrats." See Howells to William Cooper Howells, February 2, 1890, I, 417.

13. Herbert Marcuse, *One-Dimensional Man: Studies in the Ideology of Advanced Industrial Society* (Boston: Beacon, 1964), 50.

14. Herbert Marcuse, *An Essay on Liberation* (Boston: Beacon, 1969), pp. 7–8.

15. Edward Wagenknecht, *William Dean Howells: The Friendly Eye* (New York: Oxford University Press, 1969), p. 259.

16. William Dean Howells, *A Traveller from Altruria*, in *The Altrurian Romances*, ed. Clara and Rudolf Kirk (Bloomington: Indiana University Press, 1968), p. 28. All subsequent references to *The Altrurian Romances* will be from this edition and will be included parenthetically in the text.

17. William Dean Howells, "Are We a Plutocracy?" *North American Review* 158 (February 1894): 194.

18. Ibid.

19. Ibid.

20. Ibid., pp. 191, 196.

21. See William F. Ekstrom, "The Equalitarian Principle of William Dean Howells," *American Literature* 24 (March 1952): 40.

22. See Louis J. Budd, "William Dean Howells' Debt to Tolstoy," *American Slavic and East European Review* 9 (December 1950): 292–301.

23. William Dean Howells, "Who Are Our Brethren?" *Century* 60 (April 1896): 935.

24. William Dean Howells, "Equality as the Basis of Good Society," *Century* 60 (November 1895): 64.

25. Marcuse, *One-Dimensional Man*, pp. 4–5.

26. Edwin H. Cady, *The Realist at War: The Mature Years 1885–1920 of William Dean Howells* (Syracuse: Syracuse University Press, 1958), p. 153.

27. Jay Martin, *Harvests of Change: American Literature 1865–1914* (Englewood Cliffs, N.J.: Prentice-Hall, 1967), p. 228.

28. Howells, "Equality," p. 67.

29. William Dean Howells, *A Hazard of New Fortunes*, ed. Van Wyck Brooks (1890; rpt. New York: Bantam, 1960), p. 161.
30. Ibid., p. 379.
31. Marcuse, *One-Dimensional Man*, pp. 8–9.
32. Ibid., p. 12.
33. Cady, *Realist at War*, p. 198, says "the fantasy of Altruria is used here as a foil for the United States. Once again the issue most in question is the American Dream. Altruria glows in the distance as the standard of what America might become if she were truly and thoroughly democratic."
34. Marcuse, *One-Dimensional Man*, p. 98.
35. Herbert Marcuse, "Repressive Tolerance," in *A Critique of Pure Tolerance*, by Robert Paul Wolff, Barrington Moore, Jr., and Herbert Marcuse (Boston: Beacon, 1969), p. 111.
36. Ibid., p. 109.
37. Marcuse, *Essay on Liberation*, p. 68.
38. David Bleich, "Eros and Bellamy," *American Quarterly* 16 (Fall 1964): 448, compares Marcuse and Edward Bellamy and writes that Marcuse's ideas have imbued Bellamy's "*Looking Backward*, and perhaps many other utopian works, with an exciting and unprecedented relevance."
39. Howells to Charles Eliot Norton, April 15, 1907, in *Life in Letters*, II, 242.

6. Inner Death and Freedom in Henry James

1. Daniel J. Schneider, "The Divided Self in the Fiction of Henry James," *P.M.L.A.* 90 (May 1975): 447.
2. L. C. Knights, "Henry James and Human Liberty," *Sewanee Review* 83 (Winter 1975): 10–18, discusses both *The Portrait of a Lady* and *Washington Square* in terms of the themes of liberty and domination. Also, Frederick Hoffman, "Freedom and Conscious Form," discusses the "American self" as an "exploring self" and how this results in a search for form in the characters in James' works.
3. See F. O. Matthiessen, *Henry James: The Major Phase* (1944; rpt. New York: Oxford University Press, 1963), pp. 131–151.
4. William Veeder, *Henry James—the Lessons of the Master: Popular Fiction and Personal Style in the Nineteenth Century* (Chicago: University of Chicago Press, 1975), p. 10.
5. F. O. Matthiessen and Kenneth B. Murdock, eds., *The Notebooks of Henry James* (1947; rpt. New York: Oxford University Press, 1961), p. 47.
6. Henry James, *The Art of the Novel: Critical Prefaces* (New York: Charles Scribner's Sons, 1962), p. 59.

7. John L. Kimmey, "*The Bostonians* and *The Princess Casamassima*," *Texas Studies in Literature and Language* 9 (Winter 1968): 537, says, "The strongest single literary influence on Henry James during the writing of *The Princess Casamassima* in 1885 was . . . his own novel *The Bostonians*, being serialized that year in the *Century Magazine*." Kimmey goes on to note how sources from James' letters and notebooks indicate "how earnestly in his story of London low life he was struggling to avoid the kind of popular and artistic failure he had suffered in his 'American tale.'"

8. Henry James to William James, October 9, 1885, quoted by Alfred Habegger, ed., in the appendix to James' *The Bostonians* (Indianapolis: Bobbs-Merrill, 1976), p. 438.

9. James to William Dean Howells, January 2, 1888, quoted by Habegger in *The Bostonians*, p. 441.

10. Trilling, *Liberal Imagination*, p. 75.

11. See J. A. Ward, "The Ambiguities of Henry James," *Sewanee Review* 83 (Winter 1975): 56.

12. Ward further states that in James "the free person is free from fixed ideas, at least relatively free, and is, for that reason, terribly alone in his predicament; the life of freedom is necessarily experimental, necessarily more perilous than that of the life of comfortable convictions; the life of freedom invites inconsistencies and blundering" (ibid., p. 49).

13. Ward says of the relationship between James' theory of fiction and of life that "James's theory of fiction is very much a theory of life, as his aesthetic values are inseparable from his human values. The ideals of individual freedom, the cultivation of sensibility, the stress on the problems of reconciling the free self with a controlling form, the insistence on the rich variety of life, and the abhorrence of general rules—these ideas are fundamental in James to both the creating of art and living of life" (ibid., p. 45).

14. Henry James, "The Art of Fiction," in *The Future of the Novel: Essays on the Art of Fiction*, ed. Leon Edel (New York: Vintage, 1956), p. 26.

15. Henry James, "A Letter to the Deerfield Summer School," in *Future of the Novel*, p. 29.

16. James, *Art of the Novel*, p. 45.

17. Trilling, *Liberal Imagination*, p. 18.

18. Ibid., pp. 13, 11.

19. See William McMurray, "Pragmatic Realism in *The Bostonians*," *Nineteenth-Century Fiction* 16 (March 1962): 340.

20. See Gordon Pirie, *Henry James* (London: Evans Brothers, 1974), p. 96, for a discussion of James' "higher view of man's moral liberty and his independence of the physical conditions in which he lives."

21. Ibid., p. 88.

22. See Pirie's discussion of the role of media and publicity in *The Bostonians* (ibid., pp. 89–90).
23. See Jacques Ellul, *Propaganda: The Formation of Men's Attitudes* (1965; rpt. New York: Vintage, 1973), for a contemporary sociological study that still retains a moral and humanistic perspective on the subject of media and culture.
24. Trilling, *Opposing Self*, p. 112, says, "By choosing a Southerner for his hero James gained an immediate and immeasurable advantage. By this one stroke he set his story beyond any danger of seeming to be a mere bicker between morbid women and stupid men, the subject of dull, ill-natured jokes. When he involved the feminist movement with even a late adumbration of the immense tragic struggle between North and South, he made it plain that his story had to do with cultural crisis."
25. James, *The Bostonians*, p. 426.
26. Habegger, introduction to *The Bostonians*, p. xxviii. On p. xxix he says, "The novel says that life in the United States is best understood as a war between two camps, the freaks and the fascists."
27. Henry James, *The Princess Casamassima* (1886; rpt. New York: Harper Perennial, 1968), p. 48. All subsequent references to this novel will be to this edition and will be included parenthetically in the text.
28. Trilling, *Liberal Imagination*, p. 91.
29. Ibid., pp. 91–92.
30. Habegger, introduction to *The Bostonians*, p. xxxv notes that in *Maisie* "James turned inward" in order "to record someone's inner vision of events rather than the events themselves."
31. Abigail Ann Hamblen, "Henry James and the Power of Eros: *What Maisie Knew*," *The Midwest Quarterly* 9 (Summer 1968): 391.
32. Critics who tend in varying degrees to defend Maisie's innocence or moral triumph include Walter Isle, *Experiments in Form: Henry James's Novels, 1896–1901* (Cambridge, Mass.: Harvard University Press, 1968), p. 164; Muriel G. Shine, *The Fictional Children of Henry James* (Chapel Hill: University of North Carolina Press, 1969), p. 122; J. A. Ward, *The Search for Form: Studies in the Structure of James's Fiction* (Chapel Hill: University of North Carolina Press, 1967), pp. 162–163; F. R. Leavis, "James's *What Maisie Knew*: A Disagreement," *Scrutiny* 17 (Summer 1950): 115–127; and James W. Gargano, "*What Maisie Knew*: The Evolution of a 'Moral Sense,'" in *Henry James: Modern Judgments*, ed. Tony Tanner (London: Macmillan, 1968), p. 233. Other critics who question her innocence and tend to see different degrees of corruption in her include Harris W. Wilson, "What *Did* Maisie Know?" *College English* 17 (February 1956): 281; Oscar Cargill, *The Novels of Henry James* (New York: Macmillan, 1961), pp. 256, 257; Edward W. Wasiolek, "Maisie: Pure or Corrupt?" *College English* 22 (December 1960): 167, 171–172;

Marius Bewley, *The Complex Fate* (London: Chatto and Windus, 1952), p. 130; and John C. McCloskey, "What Maisie Knows: A Study of Childhood and Adolescence," *American Literature* 36 (January 1965): 513.

33. Martha Banta, "The Quality of Experience in *What Maisie Knew*," *The New England Quarterly* 42 (December 1969): 510.
34. James, *Art of the Novel*, p. 146.
35. Henry James, *What Maisie Knew* (New York: Doubleday Anchor, 1954), p. 52. All subsequent references to this novel will be from this reproduction of the 1908 New York edition and will be included parenthetically in the text.
36. James to Howard Sturgis, August 5, 1914, quoted in Knights, "Henry James and Human Liberty," p. 1.

7. Charles Ives: A Modern Perversion of Transcendentalism

1. Donal Henahan, "Danbury Discovers Ives on Centennial," New York *Times*, July 5, 1974, p. 12, cols. 1–4.
2. Quoted in David Wooldridge, *From the Steeples and Mountains: A Study of Charles Ives* (New York: Alfred A. Knopf, 1974), p. 215.
3. Ives' family history and background contributed to his interest in American themes and innovative approaches to music. He was born in Danbury, Connecticut, on October 20, 1874, and his ancestors had first settled in Connecticut in 1638 after arriving in Boston in 1635. His father, George Ives, led one of the best small village cornet bands in New England and had received the compliments of President Lincoln for his leadership of an Army band in the Civil War. Ives got some of his interest in musical daring from his father, who experimented with creating echo imitations and with achieving new sounds from pianos and violins. Like his great-grandfather and many of his other relatives, Ives graduated from Yale, where he studied music under Horatio Parker.
4. Frank R. Rossiter, *Charles Ives and His America* (New York: Liveright, 1975), p. xiii. See also H. Wiley Hitchcock and Vivian Perlis, eds., *An Ives Celebration: Papers and Panels of the Charles Ives Centennial Festival-Conference* (Urbana: University of Illinois Press, 1977).
5. See Wooldridge, *From the Steeples and Mountains*, pp. 182, 255–256. Also, through his wife Ives did have a real connection with Twain. In 1908 Ives married Harmony Twichell, the daughter of Joseph H. Twichell, a Hartford minister and close friend of Twain's. During the courtship, Ives met Twain in New York to receive his blessing for the marriage. The couple adopted one daughter.
6. Virgil Thomson, "The Ives Case," *The New York Review of Books*, May 21, 1970, p. 10.
7. Wooldridge, *From the Steeples and Mountains*, p. 4. Rosalie Sandra

Perry, *Charles Ives and the American Mind* (Kent: Kent State University Press, 1974), p. 19.

8. Henry and Sidney Cowell, *Charles Ives and His Music* (1955; rpt. New York: Oxford University Press, 1969), p. 82.

9. Charles Ives, *Essays Before a Sonata, The Majority and Other Writings*, ed. Howard Boatright (New York: Norton Library, 1970), p. 51. All subsequent references to Ives' writings will be to this edition, unless otherwise noted, and will be included parenthetically in the text.

10. Rossiter, *Charles Ives and His America*, pp. 171–172. It should be noted, however, that Perry, in *Charles Ives and the American Mind*, takes a very different view of Ives' interest in James' stream of consciousness and in the ideas of pragmatism and realism. Thus, Perry says, "The technique that Ives uses to explore the subjective is the same technique that many authors of realistic fiction used in their attempts to unravel the complexities and multiplicities of experience. For the realists, the truth is complex, and life is a complicated and ambiguous affair. The best way to express this theme was to create a work of interwoven, entangled physical density. This represented the complexity of experience. At the same time the work should contain multiple points of view to express the simultaneous existence of different levels of reality" (p. 60). Furthermore, contradicting Rossiter, Perry says, "Ives, an extremely well-read person, may have realized the implications of pragmatic thought from Oliver W. Holmes, William James, and Hermann L. F. Helmholtz" (p. 107).

11. Cowell and Cowell, *Charles Ives and His Music*, p. 54.

12. Ibid., pp. 55–56.

13. Ibid., pp. 57, 59.

14. Wooldridge, *From the Steeples and Mountains*, p. 102. See also pp. 123, 128–129.

15. Cowell and Cowell, *Charles Ives and His Music*, p. 62.

16. According to the Cowells, with an excess of $49 million in insurance sold at the time of his retirement, Ives could have been "many times a millionaire" (ibid., p. 119). Instead, he chose to live on a far smaller income. Boatright, ed., *Essays Before a Sonata, The Majority and Other Writings*, p. 139, notes Ives' belief that a personal income in excess of $100,000 should be considered a "social crime." Also, Wooldridge, *From the Steeples and Mountains*, pp. 195–196, says Ives "decided to limit his personal income to his actual needs— some said $10,000 a year, some $20,000."

17. Wooldridge, *From the Steeples and Mountains*, p. 185.

18. Ibid., p. 204.

19. See Cowell and Cowell, *Charles Ives and His Music*, pp. 135–136.

20. Wooldridge, *From the Steeples and Mountains*, p. 205.

8. Beyond the Diver Complex: The Dynamics of Modern Individualism in F. Scott Fitzgerald

1. Alan Trachtenberg, introduction to *Critics of Culture: Literature and Society in the Early Twentieth Century*, ed. Alan Trachtenberg (New York: John Wiley & Sons, 1976), p. 5.
2. Robert Sklar, introduction to *The Plastic Age (1917–1930)*, ed. Robert Sklar (New York: George Braziller, 1970), pp. 13–14.
3. Sklar says, "In mass culture the old roadblocks to social mobility came down. You could change your name, ignore your religion, leave your background a thousand miles behind. But you could never afford to neglect your appearance. In the Twenties Americans began their grand obsession with cosmetics. The absence of body odor mattered more than the lack of a family tree" (ibid., p. 17).
4. Arthur Mizener, introduction to *F. Scott Fitzgerald: A Collection of Critical Essays*, ed. Arthur Mizener, Twentieth Century Views (Englewood Cliffs, N.J.: Prentice-Hall, 1963), p. 7.
5. Trilling, "F. Scott Fitzgerald," in *Liberal Imagination*; rpt. in *F. Scott Fitzgerald*, ed. Mizener, pp. 15–16, says that "Fitzgerald was perhaps the last notable writer to affirm the Romantic fantasy, descended from the Renaissance, of personal ambition and heroism, of life committed to, or thrown away for, some ideal of self."
6. Robert Sklar, *F. Scott Fitzgerald: The Last Laocoön* (Oxford: Oxford University Press, 1967), p. 149.
7. In intensity and sincerity Fitzgerald's effort compares to similar projects by John Dewey and others. Dewey, *Individualism Old and New*, pp. 32, 33, says "the deepest problem of our times" involved the "creation of a new individualism as significant for modern conditions as the old individualism at its best was for its day and place."
8. Ibid., p. 18.
9. Fitzgerald to Maxwell Perkins, October 22, 1936, in *The Letters of F. Scott Fitzgerald*, ed. Andrew Turnbull (New York: Dell Laurel Edition, 1966), p. 296. Hereafter cited as *Letters*.
10. Fitzgerald to Francis Scott Fitzgerald, July 1938, *Letters*, p. 50.
11. Fitzgerald to Maxwell Perkins, January 19, 1933, *Letters*, p. 254.
12. Fitzgerald to Frances Scott Fitzgerald, March 15, 1940, *Letters*, pp. 80–81.
13. Andrew Turnbull, *Scott Fitzgerald* (New York: Charles Scribner's Sons, 1962), p. 227.
14. Sklar, *F. Scott Fitzgerald*, p. 57.
15. Alan Trachtenberg, "The Journey Back: Myth and History in *Tender Is the Night*," in *Experience in the Novel: Selected Papers from the English Institute*, ed. Roy Harvey Pearce (New York: Columbia University Press, 1968), pp. 133–162, discusses Sartre's views on literature, fiction, and myth, especially in *What Is Literature?* as a

means for further understanding the relationship of these forces in the Fitzgerald novel.

16. Jean-Paul Sartre, *Existential Psychoanalysis*, trans. Hazel E. Barnes, introduction by Rollo May (1943; rpt. Chicago: Gateway–Henry Regnery, 1969), p. 37. Subsequent references to this essay will be from this reprint of the original version, which appeared in *Being and Nothingness*, and will be included parenthetically in the text as *EP*. Sartre believes that his method of existential psychoanalysis differs from other methods of analysis that abstract and objectify the individual into "a sort of interdeterminate clay which would have to receive [desires] passively—or . . . be reduced to the simple bundle of these irreducible drives or tendencies. In either case the *man* disappears; we can no longer find '*the one*' to *whom* this or that experience has *happened*; either in looking for the *person*, we encounter a useless, contradictory metaphysical substance—or else the being whom we seek vanishes in a dust of phenomena bound together by external connections" (*EP*, p. 28).

17. Sartre maintains that this analysis of the meaning of the idea of "mine" involves a "double relation of consciousness" (*EP*, p. 64). John Wild, *The Challenge of Existentialism* (Bloomington: Indiana University Press, 1966), pp. 57–72, 90–95, studies Sartre's "phenomenological method" of analyzing "the concrete data of experience" and both criticizes and praises "the Sartrian dialectic" concerning awareness, consciousness, and nothingness. See also Hazel E. Barnes, *Humanistic Existentialism: The Literature of Possibility* (1959; rpt. Lincoln: University of Nebraska Press, 1967), pp. 275–362, for a discussion of Sartre's existential psychoanalysis, including a comparison of his views and ways with those of Erich Fromm and Karen Horney.

18. Arthur Mizener, appendix B, General Plan for *Tender Is the Night* in his *The Far Side of Paradise* (Boston: Houghton Mifflin, 1965), p. 345.

19. Zelda Fitzgerald's first collapse occurred in April 1930, four years before the publication of the first version of *Tender Is the Night*. Sartre, of course, did not publish *Being and Nothingness*, which included *Existential Psychoanalysis*, until 1943. The work was not translated until much later, and Fitzgerald gives no indication of any awareness of Sartre's work during the thirties. Nancy Milford, *Zelda: A Biography* (New York: Harper & Row, 1970), pp. 147–338, discusses Zelda's breakdown as well as the work of her psychiatrists in greater detail than do Fitzgerald's major biographers. Milford, pp. 179–180, quotes and paraphrases Fitzgerald's letter to Zelda's parents, Judge and Mrs. Sayre, December 1, 1930, in which he discusses the "professional standing" and opinions of both Doctor Oscar Forel, director of the sanitarium near Geneva where Zelda was a patient, and Doctor Eugene Bleuler of Zurich. The most famous consultant in Zelda's case, Doctor Bleuler, who worked with Jung

and knew Freud, helped develop the basis for a rudimentary phenomenological approach to psychoanalysis in his seminal work on naming and treating schizophrenia. Although Fitzgerald demonstrates no detailed knowledge of this work, in his letter to the Sayres he stressed Bleuler's comment that "this is something that began about five years ago. Let us hope it is only a process of re-adjustment. Stop blaming yourself. You might have retarded it but you couldn't have prevented it." In a letter to Zelda, March 19, 1940, *Letters*, p. 131, Fitzgerald mentions both Doctor Forel and Doctor Adolph Meyer, director of the Henry Phipps Psychiatric Clinic of Johns Hopkins University. The technical nature of the doctors' work and Fitzgerald's limited access to them would seem to diminish their influence on his thinking about psychoanalysis. Doctor Bleuler is mentioned throughout a basic reader on existential and phenomenological psychoanalysis, *Existence*, ed. Rollo May, Ernest Angel, and Henri F. Ellenberger (New York: Clarion, 1958), as well as in Ernest Jones, *The Life and Work of Sigmund Freud*, ed. Lionel Trilling and Steven Marcus, abridged edition (Garden City: Anchor, 1961). However, others, including Eugene Minkowski and Ludwig Binswanger, seem to have exerted greater influence on these areas of psychiatry than did Zelda's famous doctor. In an interesting article that compares Fitzgerald's approach to that of a form of social psychology, Lee M. Whitehead, "*Tender Is the Night* and George Herbert Mead: An 'Actor's' Tragedy," *Literature and Psychology* 15 (Summer 1965); rpt. in Marvin J. LaHood, ed., *Tender Is the Night: Essays in Criticism* (Bloomington: Indiana University Press, 1969), p. 167, finds that "to an astonishing extent Fitzgerald thinks about his characters in terms explicitly similar" to the social psychology of George Herbert Mead. Diver fails, he says, because of "an inability to adapt successfully to a social milieu for which his upbringing has not prepared him."
20. Nathaniel Hawthorne, "Ethan Brand," in *Nathaniel Hawthorne: Selected Tales and Sketches*, ed. Hyatt H. Waggoner (New York: Rinehart Edition, 1964), pp. 313–314.
21. Ibid., p. 314.
22. F. Scott Fitzgerald, *Tender Is the Night*, rev. ed., introduction by Malcolm Cowley (New York: Charles Scribner's Sons, 1951), p. 30. Subsequent references to this edition will be included parenthetically in the text.
23. D. W. Harding, "Mechanisms of Misery," in *F. Scott Fitzgerald*, ed. Mizener, p. 145, discusses Diver's isolation.
24. Kent and Gretchen Kreuter, "The Moralism of the Later Fitzgerald," in *Tender Is the Night: Essays in Criticism*, p. 53, discuss "moral decline" in the novel.
25. Nathaniel Hawthorne, "Young Goodman Brown," in *Selected Tales and Sketches*, pp. 121, 122.
26. Paul F. Schmidt, *Rebelling, Loving and Liberation: A Metaphysics*

of the Concrete (Albuquerque: Hummingbird Press, 1971), p. 17, describes Sartre's vital term, "being-for-itself," as "a being which never is anything but is always becoming and as becoming so always negating yet simultaneously creating; a being which since it is not fixed *in* its being, is therefore sheer contingency." John Wild, *Challenge of Existentialism*, pp. 77, 161, defines the *en soi* as "non-human reality" that lacks "all power and potency" and the "human *pour soi*" as "purely potential nothingness . . . which literally makes its world."

27. See Jean-Paul Sartre, *Between Existentialism and Marxism* (New York: Pantheon, 1974). See Robert Denoon Cumming, ed., *The Philosophy of Jean-Paul Sartre* (New York: Vintage, 1965), pp. 415–483, for a good abridgment of Sartre's *Critique of Dialectical Reason*. For valuable essays on Sartre's political philosophy and its relationship to Marxism, see Mary Warnock, ed., *Sartre: A Collection of Critical Essays* (New York: Anchor, 1971). For a famous attack on Sartre's attempt to bridge Marxism and existentialism, see Georg Lukács, "Existentialism," in *Marxism and Human Liberation: Essays on History, Culture and Revolution by Georg Lukács*, ed. E. San Juan, Jr. (New York: Delta, 1973), pp. 243–266.

28. Milton Stern, *The Golden Moment: The Novels of F. Scott Fitzgerald* (Urbana: University of Illinois Press, 1970), p. 329. In contrast, for a critic who approaches Fitzgerald and *Tender Is the Night* from a politically radical viewpoint, see John F. Callahan, *The Illusions of a Nation: Myth and History in the Novels of F. Scott Fitzgerald* (Urbana: University of Illinois Press, 1972).

29. See Stern, *Golden Moment*, p. 332.

30. Kay House of San Francisco State pointed out the ambiguity involved in this sentence.

31. See, for example, John O. Stark, *The Literature of Exhaustion: Borges, Nabokov and Barth* (Durham: Duke University Press, 1974), and John Barth, "The Literature of Exhaustion," *Atlantic*, August 1967, pp. 29–34; rpt. in *The American Novel since World War II*, ed. Marcus Klein (New York: Fawcett, 1969), pp. 267–279.

32. F. Scott Fitzgerald, *The Crack-Up*, ed. Edmund Wilson (New York: New Directions, 1956), pp. 76, 75.

33. Ibid., p. 69.

34. Ibid., p. 70.

35. Edmund Wilson, foreword to *The Last Tycoon*, by F. Scott Fitzgerald (New York: Charles Scribner's Sons, 1970), p. x.

36. Arthur Mizener, "The Maturity of Scott Fitzgerald," *Sewanee Review* 67 (Autumn 1959): 658–675; rpt. in *F. Scott Fitzgerald*, ed. Mizener, p. 166.

37. Fitzgerald, *The Last Tycoon*, p. 108.

38. Ibid., pp. 58, 125.

39. Michael Wood, *America in the Movies* (New York: Basic Books, 1975), p. 172.
40. Jean-Paul Sartre, *Anti-Semite and Jew*, trans. George Becker (1948; rpt. New York: Schocken Books, 1965), pp. 53, 54.
41. Fitzgerald, *The Last Tycoon*, p. 131.
42. See Mizener, *Far Side of Paradise*, p. 330, and Turnbull, *Scott Fitzgerald*, p. 307.
43. See William James, "Pragmatism and Humanism," in *Pragmatism and Other Essays*, ed. Joseph L. Blau (New York: Washington Square Press, 1963), pp. 105–108.
44. William James, "What Pragmatism Means," in *Pragmatism and Other Essays*, pp. 35–37.
45. Fitzgerald, *The Crack-Up*, p. 69.
46. Ibid., p. 84.
47. Ibid., p. 81.
48. Ibid., pp. 81–82.
49. Ibid., pp. 82, 83.
50. Fitzgerald to Frances Scott Fitzgerald, June 12, 1940, *Letters*, p. 96.
51. Fitzgerald to Frances Scott Fitzgerald, October 5, 1940, *Letters*, p. 114.
52. Fitzgerald, *The Crack-Up*, p. 302.

9. The Radical Individualism of William James: A Theory of Experience and the Self for Today

1. Hoffman, "Dogmatic Innocence," pp. 114–115.
2. Ibid., p. 115.
3. Hoffman further maintains that James' arguments are "an act of desperation; the major concern is to restore to the self the possibilities that it may guarantee its continuity in time, that such a continuance of conscious being is a supreme responsibility (a 'dreadful freedom,' as the existentialists put it) of a conative being" (ibid., pp. 118, 115).
4. Hoffman, "William James and the Modern Literary Consciousness," further states, "The results of his analysis of the self pushed James further and further away from science itself and toward a transcendent affirmation of the self that seems a mixture of exasperation and nostalgia."
5. See Quentin Anderson, "Practical and Visionary Americans," *The American Scholar* 45 (Summer 1976): 406, 408.
6. Ibid., pp. 408, 406, 417.
7. William Barrett, "Our Contemporary, William James," *Commentary*, December 1975, p. 55.
8. See Gay Wilson Allen, *William James: A Biography* (New York: Viking, 1967); John Wild, *The Radical Empiricism of William James* (New

York: Doubleday Anchor, 1970); Rollo May, "William James' Humanism and the Problem of Will," in *William James: Unfinished Business*, ed. Robert MacLeod (Washington, D.C.: American Psychological Association, 1969); and Rollo May, *Love and Will* (New York: Norton, 1969).

9. William James, "Monistic Idealism," *A Pluralistic Universe*, in *Essays in Radical Empiricism and A Pluralistic Universe*, ed. Ralph Barton Perry, introduction by Richard J. Bernstein (New York: Dutton, 1971), p. 150. All future references to essays included in *Essays in Radical Empiricism* (1912) or *A Pluralistic Universe* (1909) will be to this edition of both works and will be included parenthetically in the text and cited as *ERE* and *PU*.

10. William James, "Humanism and Truth," in his *The Meaning of Truth: A Sequel to Pragmatism*, introduction by Ralph Ross (1909; rpt. Ann Arbor: University of Michigan Press, 1970), p. 92.

11. Ibid.

12. William James, "Is Life Worth Living?" in *Essays on Faith and Morals*, p. 31.

13. Ibid., p. 30.

14. Ibid., pp. 30, 29, 30.

15. William James, *The Varieties of Religious Experience: A Study in Human Nature* (New York: Modern Library, 1902), p. 492. All subsequent references to this book will be to this edition and will be included parenthetically in the text and cited as *VRE*.

16. Slotkin, *Regeneration through Violence*, p. 103.

17. James, "The Will to Believe," in *Essays on Faith and Morals*, pp. 32–33.

18. Daniel Bell, *The Cultural Contradictions of Capitalism* (New York: Basic Books, 1976), pp. 28–29, 30.

19. See George R. Garrison and Edward H. Madden, "William James—Warts and All," *American Quarterly* 29 (Summer 1977): 207–221.

10. After the Sixties: The Continuing Search

1. See Marshall Berman, *The Politics of Authenticity: Radical Individualism and the Emergence of Modern Society* (New York: Atheneum, 1972), p. 35.

2. Eugene J. McCarthy, "A Note on the New Equality," *Commentary*, November 1977, p. 55.

3. Saul Bellow, *Mr. Sammler's Planet* (New York: Viking Compass, 1973), p. 280. All subsequent references to this novel will be to this edition and will be included parenthetically in the text.

4. Wood, *America in the Movies*, pp. 28, 32, 33.

5. Marshall McLuhan, *The Mechanical Bride: Folklore of Industrial Man* (Boston: Beacon, 1951), p. 97.

6. Marshall McLuhan, "American Advertising," *Horizon*, October 1947, pp. 132–141; rpt. in *Mass Culture*, pp. 436, 438, 442.
7. Marshall McLuhan, "Sight, Sound, and the Fury," *Commonweal* 60 (April 1954): 168–197; rpt. in *Mass Culture*, p. 495.
8. Marshall McLuhan, *The Gutenberg Galaxy: The Making of Typographic Man* (1962; rpt. New York: Signet, 1969), p. 319.
9. Ibid., p. 328.
10. Ibid., pp. 329, 328, 329.
11. Morris Eaves, "Blake and the Artistic Machine: An Essay in Decorum and Technology," *P.M.L.A.* 92 (October 1977): 903.
12. McLuhan, *Mechanical Bride*, p. 144.
13. Trilling, *Sincerity and Authenticity*, pp. 171–172.
14. Berlin, *Four Essays on Liberty*, pp. 108–109.
15. Ibid., pp. 138–139.
16. Emerson, "The American Scholar," I, 100.
17. James, "What Pragmatism Means," pp. 23, 37.
18. Ibid., p. 32.
19. Berlin, *Four Essays on Liberty*, p. 171.
20. Ibid., p. 172.
21. John Dewey, *Freedom and Culture* (1939; rpt. New York: Capricorn, 1963), p. 124.
22. Ibid., pp. 173, 174.

Index